BEYOND
THE
BROKEN MARRIAGE

BEYOND THE BROKEN MARRIAGE

by
Larry M. Correu

THE WESTMINSTER PRESS
Philadelphia

BOOK DESIGN BY ALICE DERR

First edition

Published by The Westminster Press®
Philadelphia, Pennsylvania

PRINTED IN THE UNITED STATES OF AMERICA
9 8 7 6 5 4 3 2 1

Library of Congress Cataloging in Publication Data

Correu, Larry M., 1931–
   Beyond the broken marriage.

   Bibliography: p.
   1. Divorce—Psychological aspects. I. Title.
HQ814.C67   1982   646.7′8   82-13661
ISBN 0-664-24446-7 (pbk.)

TO MY OLDER SON
who first filled me with the pride and joy of being "Dad," and who knows the pain of my divorce but has borne it courageously

TO MY DAUGHTER
who also has brightened this father's life, and filled a place in his heart reserved from eternity

TO MY YOUNGER SON
who came into our lives and brought heaven with him

And most of all . . .
TO MY WIFE
whose love, sacrifice, and encouragement not only have made possible the completion of this book, but who after the "funeral" has herself been the Afterlife!

Contents

Foreword

HE WALKED OUT of my room looking as though his whole world had just fallen in. The reason he looked that way was that his whole world had just fallen in.

The marriage he hoped to save was finished. Not legally yet, but finished in the two hearts where it mattered.

Remember the last time a friend shared that kind of ache and you couldn't think of thing one to say? So you cried together. That's what we did.

I've always admired Larry Correu, and there are several reasons. For one thing, he's good to look at—tall, handsome, warm smile, mysterious. But even more, he has clawed his way back up out of the valley to a position of trust and influence. Longtime editor of a devotional guide serving six denominations in the United States and Canada, he is a skilled writer. He knows his way around phrases, through stories, and especially he knows how to help those who have been hurt as he has been hurt.

Then particularly I like the way Larry keeps taking us to the mirror. That's what he does in BEYOND THE BROKEN MARRIAGE. Like Augustine, he forces us to say, "Soul, thou ailest here and here."

Makes sense, doesn't it? In any relational breakdown,

does it really matter what "they" did? Always, the healer question is, "Will *I* face up to *my* responsibility right now?"

Then, having led us to some honest introspection, Larry turns us around. "Look," he says, "off there in the distance see the mountains to climb, islands to discover, rivers to ford, new challenges, new thrills. I know," he says, "I've been there. Come off the ash heap. The Lord is calling you to better things. There is no tragedy so tragic but that he can use it. If you'll let him, he'll bring you to a better tomorrow."

That's the kind of hope this book offers.

CHARLIE W. SHEDD

Fripp Island
Frogmore, South Carolina

Introduction

YOU MAY BE READING this because separation or divorce threatens your marriage. Or it could be that your marriage already is broken. What I want to say to you most at the outset is that *I know how you feel!* I've been where you are. I've known the tearing inside when separation threatens and when separation happens. And yes, I have known the pain—and release—of divorce.

My story may be similar to yours in that I did not want my spouse to leave or to file for divorce. I am aware that many of those who do take the initiative in separating or filing do so reluctantly. Yet the special slant of the pages to come is toward those for whom divorce is perhaps unthinkable and for whom the prospect or reality of it is a literal terror.

Most clergypersons are called upon to counsel with those in the throes of marriage collapse. But I look upon my personal struggles through and beyond a broken marriage as a special asset. I believe I have been and can be of help especially to those facing unwanted separation or divorce. That's why I have written this book.

What I share I have shared before in one way or another with any number of maritally troubled persons who were experiencing what you may be experiencing.

Many times their own insights about coping with their marital crises have supported or sharpened my own, for which I am grateful.

As you read, I would like you to feel that you and I are sitting down together, too, and sharing in a personal way. I hope you will sense the binding tie that I and countless others who have walked the way you are walking now hold with you. I hope we can communicate in the confidence of really knowing how we feel.

Please keep in mind that while you may go through most of what is shared here, your story could unfold differently. The order in which you feel certain emotions or face certain choices or stages could be entirely unique for you. Your need for my suggestions or for facing what you are going through may be on a different time schedule altogether. Still, it remains that so much we hold in common runs through all we experience. That's why we can be of help to each other.

My fervent wish is that you will see that you too can move beyond the trauma of an unwanted broken marriage. What I desire for you is that you will find, as others have found, that out of your struggles can come a new sense of being in touch with life and meaning, a new courage for continuing—even, if need be, in a life apart from the other. All along the way, please be assured that I hold you in my prayers.

In writing, I have also thought a good bit about those who helped me when I needed it most. Their prayerful support, counsel, and words of hope came to me as God's caring, strength, and guidance. I hold them in my prayers, too—very gratefully.

L. M. C.

1
Cultivating an Accepting Spirit

I DOUBT THAT ANYONE suspected just how troubled my marriage was, least of all myself, until it was very late. When separation finally came, it was all so unreal. It was like some ghostly drama cast with paper-thin people. It seemed as though I was standing off and watching me in what was happening, without being in it at all. Facing the reality of the situation became my foremost need and most difficult challenge. And, if your marriage is on the verge of or in the process of dying, accepting the reality of your situation likely will be *your* need and challenge, too.

I do not know the specifics of why your marriage is failing, of course. You may be the victim of a triangle, in which your spouse has become involved with another. Your marriage partner may be too much a child to be able to endure the responsibilities of a lasting marriage. Your spouse may be a mentally ill person who has made entirely impossible the interaction that is necessary for any strong relationship, while at the same time irrationally holding you responsible for everything. Or you may be in a situation in which the emotional needs of both yourself and your spouse have been too great to feed the life of the marriage. Again, you could be one of myriads of spouses who suddenly are faced with the bold announcement: "I don't love you anymore!"

There are so many situations out of which marriage breakdown results. Whatever the specifics for you, the progression of events to what they are now may or may not translate into divorce. But it is *terribly* important for you to begin accepting not only how troubled the marriage is, but that the *death* of your marriage is a possibility.

Sure, it would be easier to go on living in a paper-thin world, refusing to be touched by what is stark and real. It could be less painful never to face the fact that a "cancer" is on your marriage. But there just isn't any sense to a make-believe approach to your crisis. You can't pretend it away. Nor can you, by minimizing or wishing, change the way your spouse now perceives of or feels about you or the marriage.

You may want with all your heart to "keep" the departed spouse. You may feel compelled to wish or entice—or even coerce—your spouse into some kind of pact or trap that will *assure* the continuation of your marriage. The imaginary "Peter Pumpkin Eater" may have been able to manage something like that with his straying spouse; but it is unlikely that you will come up with a pumpkin shell scheme that will contain yours "very well" for long, if your spouse does not want to be kept.

All the pretending in the world is not going to work any miracles. So it is no use wasting time or energy straining against or shutting out the way things are. If your marriage is "on the rocks," it's time to pull in, to pull up, to gather in your will and your emotions. You don't want to deny your hurt, or what you feel or hope for, any more than you deny what the marriage has come to. You do need to call forth the best, most realistic attitude you can. Sure it's difficult. It's downright suffocating. Tragic and harsh. It hurts and bleeds and pinches at you. But, facing the "ugliness" as best as you can is your saving hope. *It is time to muster your best, accepting spirit!*

How do you do that? Consider these suggestions, which helped me tremendously as I stumbled along. In a sense, all the ideas in this book point toward an accepting, courageous spirit. I frame these special few at the outset with the sincerest hope that your way from this point on may become steadier.

1. *Keep in mind that the separation may be what your spouse needs most at present—space and time for reflective withdrawal from you, from the marriage.* You can be more accepting and patient in your dilemma if you remember that the best hope for reconciliation is to give your spouse just that: space and time. Depending on what the circumstances are with your spouse and surrounding the departure, your ability to leave your spouse alone at this point could be crucial. While there may be times when you do make contact, haggling or begging will only set back any hope of meaningful communication between you. The old adage about "one day at a time" is helpful here. The anxious pull toward trying to push or beg the spouse's return can be better lived with and controlled if you resolve each day to be as calm and patient as you can, just for that day. Even if there is little doubt about the finality of the spouse's decision to stay separated, a day at a time, hands-off, collected approach will be saving for you, anyway.

If leaving your husband or wife alone is a special problem for you, as it understandably might be, you may want to read Chapter 3 now, where more is shared about a hands-off policy. As you wonder and wait and pray, giving your spouse adequate time and space is the most practical, commonsense thing you can do.

2. *Focus on the practical side.* If you really can begin accepting, mentally and emotionally, "what is," you will

be able to reap the freeing effects of a steadier repose. If you can begin to accept even any inclinations of your partner to put a final end to the marriage, you will be setting the stage for the marriage to save itself, if that turns out to be at all within the realm of possibility. You also will be protecting yourself, too, from your own vulnerability. You will open the way for you to decide more wisely for your own future well-being. You will be better able to seek help for your own growth or meaning whether your partner does or not. If you are a parent, you will have more strength and presence of mind and heart, too, to lend to your offspring.

For all these reasons and perhaps more, accepting where you are in your marriage relationship is the most practical thing you can do. *It is to your best advantage.* The more composure you have, the more command of the situation. The more accepting in spirit you are, the better you will be able to work through to the most helpful solution for you, your spouse, or your children, if children were born of the union.

3. *Try some real honesty on for size.* Be as honest as you possibly can be. In spite of the disappointment you feel, is it possible that you are at least a little relieved that the festering illness of your marriage has come to a head? In your case, the honest-to-goodness answer may be (at a feeling level, anyway) a resounding "No!" No, you're not at all relieved, and how could I dare to ask. If so, I can respect and understand that. On the other hand, there is no shame if you do admit to any genuine relief by saying simply, "In some ways, I am relieved."

Certainly, at least there is a real plus, if you will be open to it, in taking this respite from the troubles you and your spouse were experiencing together as a kind of interlude, a reflective interlude. Don't you have a built-in breather here, in which you can back off and do some serious pondering about your marriage, about yourself?

Cannot this time given you—all right, thrust upon you—
be used to try to understand more honestly some of the
contributing factors to your marriage breakdown? Here's
a time for sizing up how things are with you, a time for
getting to know yourself better, at least. And can't you
welcome that honestly? Even if you feel none of the relief
mentioned above?

4. *Make your present situation produce blessings in
disguise.* Deliberately look upon and *use* your situation
to your positive good. Make it work for you. Not only is
it a time for serious reflection; isn't it a time for other
possibilities? What an opportunity for getting your fi-
nances in order, perhaps, or for seeing to that physical
examination so important to the better care of your
health. Or for doing some of the things you haven't had a
chance or the time to do before. Is this lull in your
marriage a door you can open to new decisions about
vocation, possibly? What new friends can you now
visibly take into your life, ones who are coming forward
with love and support? Isn't there a special chance at
hand to get to know old friends or family members
better? Or to let your children into your life more?

Much more can be said about children, and I will do
this in later pages. I also could suggest other blessings
that can emerge from your dilemma, but you will be able
to see these better than I. Allow your dilemma to bless
you in whatever way it will. In doing so, you are not
giving up on your marriage. Nor are you welcoming the
departure of your spouse or even approving it. You *are*
refusing to be defeated by your dilemma. You *are* helping
yourself to greater acceptance by the sheer fact that you
are gleaning positive results from it.

5. *Take courage from the fact that others have walked
this way before you.* There is strength in this thought. It
helps that others, whether their marriages ultimately
survived or not, have been exactly where you are. And

17

they have made it. The way ahead may be uncertain, the present confusing and difficult, but you too can come through this. You too can rebuild into something good and even beautiful. You too can persevere and overcome. Believing this will add to your calm and fill you with hope.

6. *Forgive and be forgiven.* More will be shared about forgiveness later. Stress now that it can pave the way to a spirit of acceptance. Where you have been hurt, seek to forgive. Wherein you have hurt, seek forgiveness. The sooner you come into an attitude of forgiveness, the sooner you will be freed from the pressures of resentment. To forgive another as God forgives you is gracious and freeing for you, for the other, for any children of the marriage. Regularly and prayerfully search your heart to clear it of enmity toward anyone who has hurt or used you. This prevents your bowing to the dictates of hate or revenge. It takes the wind out of your bucking the situation in a detrimental way. You do not need to be a pushover to have a forgiving spirit. Quite the opposite; in forgiving you have an upper hand, really, that refuses to allow the other partner to control your life. You gain more understanding and a will for the good of the other. You grow in an accepting spirit because you can act responsibly and not spitefully. The energy that would be used in begrudging frees itself to be channeled into the adjustments at hand.

The other side of the coin is to welcome the forgiveness of your spouse for you. And to learn to forgive yourself for some of the weaknesses you may uncover from your reflections about yourself or your marriage. To receive and accept the gift of forgiveness is freeing for you, for your spouse, and for the divine working within you.

The divine working? Well, you may or may not be a

person of faith. But, before we consider the area of faith, I offer another suggestion.

7. *Pick up on the business of life.* Your life doesn't come to a halt now; there are things to be done that must be done, in your work, in your daily and even routine responsibilities. Do them believing that they are in themselves therapy for you. Each endeavor, each task, moves you one step closer to a time of greater inward settlement. That time surely can come, regardless of the outcome of your marriage crisis. And, in doing what is before you, what must be done, you are, once again, refusing to be defeated, while enhancing the accepting spirit that is growing within you. Now for that suggestion about faith.

8. *Do let God into your life and into your dilemma.* If you have not been a person of faith, particularly, up to now, isn't this an opportune time to ask yourself what place faith has in your life? Contrary to what you may think, God will rejoice over a new admission from you that you need divine wisdom and strength in your crisis. Faith in God will give you courage to accept, because by faith you allow one who is beyond yourself to walk with you through the crisis. You have one to whom you can release your marriage and your spouse and your children. In thus releasing, you share your burdens, while accepting a helper and an advocate for your best interests. You trust the present and future to a will and a power greater than your own. You aren't controlling the outcome of the dilemma—not that. In fact, you are doing just the opposite. You are confessing that you are *not* God. You are admitting your lack of control of the situation. Yet without placing any designs on God, you are trusting the divine power to work in and for you. You dare to believe that there will come a day when you will look back on what is taking place and will find meaning in all this,

whether your marriage is preserved or not.

A minister friend of mine once said to me: "Larry, one day you will be able to look back and see meaning in what is happening. A person of faith believes that everything in his or her life ultimately holds meaning." My friend shared this with me as I felt the pain of separation from my spouse and my little son. It was difficult for me to "hear" at the time, difficult to hear for myself or for my son. It may be hard for you to hear it now. But if you will allow the idea to penetrate your soul, it will temper your will. It will give you courage for each day.

Yes, yes, it's possible by faith—that "out there" in the scary future, there will arrive a time, by the grace of God, when you will look back down the way you are treading with far greater insight, however your marriage pans out. There will come a day when you will look back with an eternal sense that with God the life which time has been sketching for you fits a new frame—with or without the healing of your marriage. Pray for that healing, if that is your heartfelt, sincere desire; then surrender it all to God.

What courage born of faith there is in this way. What courage there will be for you, all along the way.

As you recover from the initial shock of separation, as you reach for the control of an accepting spirit in all the ways we have shared, how I hold you in my prayers.

2
Coping with the Blow to Your Ego

IF MY OWN EXPERIENCE rings true, part of the shock you feel in the breakdown of your marriage, and part of the problem of accepting it, is that you are baring more of your humanness to others. You and those who know you have been aware that you were capable of erring and being erred against, of hurting as well as being hurt. But as it goes public that you are (really!) part of the sickness and deterioration of a marriage it could be threatening to you.

Of course there is no way to keep separation secret, at least not for very long, and certainly, not impending divorce. Sooner or later friends and family will know, probably already know, that things have come to this with you and your spouse. Most will be supportive, but some may not understand. Some may not be honest with you about their feelings. Some very likely will talk about you behind your back. You may wonder how they feel about you. Some may appear to blame you without really blaming you at all. You may feel you have let some of them down. The end result may be that your feelings about yourself are brought into question and your self-image shaken, at least for a time.

Two shock waves from the aftermath of the newsbreak

21

of my own marriage failure still tug at me, if I let them. Both illustrate, I believe, something of what you may be in for as your crisis becomes known. One of these shock waves reverberates from my announcement to the congregation I served that my wife had left me. I remember saying to them something like: "I want you to know about this from me. The situation is one of those which, however regrettable, will have to work itself out. I have discussed this with the officers of the church, and I am appreciative of their support."

I still recall some of the faces of the people in the congregation that day. Some obviously had heard; others stared in disbelief. But the face I remember most is that of a man in the second pew whose wife had left him some months before. There passed between us an instant gaze of understanding. Yet there was a flush of disappointment, too. The next day, I heard he was holed up in his mobile home, intoxicated. Apparently I was his excuse to begin drinking again!

A letter from my mother generated the second shock wave. I had broken the news to her by phone. Unbelieving, she wrote the reaction of a friend of hers: "How *could* it happen to such a *nice* person!"

In recalling the look of the alcoholic worshiper, I can still feel a sense of having let another down. He had placed faith in me; his faith in me now was shattered. And from the letter from my mother the question hovered: Am I a nice person still—now that I have joined the ranks of those to whom such things happen? For a while I think I felt the same way I did the time I was caught in a gully washer while driving on an unfamiliar road—horrified that at any moment I might be washed out!

Whatever your experiences have been or will be as the knowledge of your being part of a marriage failure is shared, if those experiences jar your ego, it may help to face these significant questions which emerge from my own ego battle.

1. *Have I been expecting too much of myself?* This invites you to take a more realistic look at your "perfectness"—or rather the lack of it. It could well be that you have had an unrealistic view of your finiteness. You may need now to let yourself down a notch in your thinking, to where you really have been all along. You always have been human. It has always been a fact that you are *not* perfect. The difference now is that in a perhaps more conspicuous or larger way your imperfection is more visible.

Really, can it be that you have been expecting more of yourself than is humanly feasible? This is not to justify your marriage dilemma or any need for forgiveness you may feel; it is meant to help you be more realistic about the turn of events. Even those whose marriages never suffer a ripple of conflict, which I doubt is possible, sooner or later must come to grips with their finiteness, through one experience or another. They, no less than you, are *not* God!

Looked at another way, to walk in this world is to err and to be touched by the errors of others. It is to wander out of the sunshine into the rain, at least some of the time. To believe otherwise is to live in a world of dreams.

Dreams! This is something of what you are going through, too, isn't it? Bursted dreams? About a happy home, about a successful, harmonious marriage? So ask yourself this question too.

2. *Have I been expecting too much of marriage itself?* Therein could have been part of the problem all along; therein may be part of the problem if you are personally devastated by the newsbreak concerning your marriage crisis. Like a lot of us, you may have staked a great deal on a dream of a happy home. If you came from a happy home, which you value very much, you may have had

23

trouble accepting even the smaller conflicts of your marriage relationship. If the home of your upbringing was not very harmonious, you may have been determined to make yours "beautiful." If by chance your parents engrained in you that marriage troubles are wrong, wrong, wrong, this cup before you could be bitter gall indeed.

Not that dreams of a happy home are wrong and out of fashion. But yours could have been lofty and idealistic enough that the drop from marriage success to marriage failure has been like pushing your ego off the Empire State Building. I think this was partly my problem. *How I wanted a happy home!* What a long, hard fall I was in for. My dream was a large one; I was part of that dream; the dream burst; I was part of the bursting. That others knew my dream had burst was double trouble. The experience itself was a harsh blow to my ego. Does any of this ring true for you?

3. *Has my life been controlled too much by what others think?* And too little by who I really am inside? A divorced woman said to me: "One of the hardest things was the neighbors. They talked too much. They just wouldn't accept it. They had to blame one or the other of us." Some of the woman's reactions were probably imagined, but feelings were genuine. The problem was, her feelings still remained with her after many years of putting separation and eventual divorce behind her. She had never quite gotten over the feeling of being put down by her neighbors. She was still controlled by what others thought.

What we are touching on here is the question of inward freedom. Are you free to be you—to bare to others your finiteness, yes, and to walk in the stormy rain if you must, without being slave to the opinions and pressures of others? Are you free to "fail" and possibly lose some of the approval of others? Yet are you free to continue to believe that you are a worthy person?

A good part of the impact you may feel could arise from the fact that your spouse is the one who wanted this separation. You wonder, perhaps: "Do others blame me for the marriage collapse? Will they be able to see the positive side of my desire to save the marriage—whatever has happened? Will they feel I am completely responsible?" My guess is that those who are friends or family will give you some credit and support, regardless of why your spouse has departed. And as they see that you now are doing the best you can, they will be prone to be even more supportive.

Another part of the impact you may feel could be a matter of truth and consequences—the fear of what others might *do* in reaction to your dilemma. For example: "Will my job be affected?" I felt that kind of pressure, admittedly more than one might, because of being in the pastoral ministry. After all, ministers are not supposed to have personal problems. Hogwash about that! In all likelihood, it is mostly hogwash about possible consequences relating to your job, or to possible rejection by friends, or whatever. Most people, I know from experience, are naturally supportive of others; those who are not—well, they need *our* support! To this day, there is a very warm place in my heart for the many who stood by me, including the marvelous congregation I served.

Not that you take your erring, your hurting of others, your hurt to yourself, as nothing at all. To do so would be obscene. The marvel is that you are free to live in this imperfect world having been marked publicly as less than a "perfect" person. You can dismantle the protective fence you have built around your ego. Though you still value the esteem of others, you *can* let their opinions come in closer and dance around you without devastating you. You *can* allow your finiteness to show. And if your marriage does go the way of the divorce statistics, you *can* weather the public knowledge of that, too.

No one truly judges you but God; not one knows what is in your heart but you and God; no one controls you but you yourself. You may feel that you are not proud of everything you may have done to contribute to your marriage breakdown, and that you could have done some things to prevent it. If so, you will be penitent about that. But you are free to choose not to let the private or public knowledge of it destroy you.

You also are free to affirm yourself. This next question will help you do just that.

4. *Am I all failure?* Of course you are not. For one thing, you are a worthy person before God. You can face your finiteness while still affirming that you possess a personal worth. That worth has been there all along. It is not taken away by the opinions of others or by the knowledge that you are finite before God. *Affirm yourself!* Affirm that God created you and "saw that it was good." Affirm that "God don't make no junk."

Basically we all are good. We are created in the image of the one who alone is goodness and love. We can walk in the stormy rain because we have enough God-given sunshine within us to hold us together. And if you don't feel that, if the rays of your basic goodness do not warm your heart at the moment, affirm it anyway. That affirmation is another ticket to freedom, another salve to the blow to your ego.

Another aspect of positive self-affirmation has to do with the times and ways you contributed to the health of the marriage. No, you are *not* all failure. There likely were, there must be some pluses to your credit. Even the heaviest offenders in marriage breakdown can claim some pluses, I feel. Dwell on those times, those bright moments when you acted, responded, gave, in such a way as to strengthen communication or bring joy into the life of your spouse. Dwell too on the fact that regardless of what has led up to the separation, you have tried to hold to your commitment to your marriage; you have not wanted the separation, you do not want a divorce. There is a certain integrity in your willingness even yet to try to effect a reconciliation, if that is your desire.

Your positive contributions to the marriage and your openness to reconciliation are likely known to others. Knowing that they know can help to temper the experience of "going public" also.

So please, hold *yourself* up prayerfully before God. Humbly, patiently, but positively, hold yourself up, with affirmation. For I believe God still affirms and appreciates you. Even as you square your shoulders, pick up the pieces of bursted dreams, and recover from whatever ego knocks you may be experiencing.

3
One Last Try

IF SAVING YOUR marriage has been your fervent hope and you are putting forth one more, last ol' college try by seeking out professional help, you are to be *commended*. For who knows, in your case maybe, counseling may lead or have already led to *another* try, on your or your spouse's part. Communication may be open again and, with continued help, the possibility of a reconciliation becomes more likely. But take care not to expect more than may be possible. Don't set yourself up for a great fall.

Too many of us expect a counselor to work miracles, according to *our* goals. The counselor's goals may be much more objective—aimed at the client's fulfillment and growth, beamed toward discovering the most workable solutions to problems. This means that, sometimes, even when the counselor tries to avoid it, a marriage may stay separated and broken whether one partner or the other wants it or not—precisely because only one partner wants it. The counselor is wise enough to know that there is little basis for lasting reconciliation, tough as that is.

Sorry, but it's true; motivation for healing your marriage relationship will have to come from both of you. You may be motivated with all your heart, but all the king's horses and all the king's men can't put your marriage back together again—much less one lone counselor doing it—*if your spouse does not truly want this.* Hence you have to consider the possibility that your "one last try" through counseling could end in disappointment.

A few weeks after my separation, I received news that my partner in marriage had agreed, *at my request,* please note, to sit down with a professional person to weigh once again the course she was taking. The counselor whom I had asked to telephone her notified me that she was keeping the appointment. I was to see the counselor the day after that. This was the respite I had hoped for. Endeavors now seemed routine. Moments of prayer became intense. Nighttime hours ran from sleep. Each waking dawn was welcomed because it moved me closer, I thought, to the time of new possibility. Then there came the appointed moment when I faced the counselor, only to hear:

"I'm sorry I have to tell you this. Your wife doesn't want to make any more appointments. We've talked at length and she's convinced separation should be permanent. She's decided divorce is the best course to take."

In retrospect, I might have known better. My resentment and disappointment nearly overwhelmed me.

So take care. Pursue the possibilities in counseling if you feel it best and wise, but walk cautiously. Full of hope, but cautiously. Steady, but not naively!

Actually, one of the purposes of counseling at this point could be to help you—apart from your spouse—to try to achieve greater inward calm. It could foster some of the acceptance of your situation I wrote about in Chapter 1. Counseling could help you quell some of the anxiety within you so that you yourself can face your dilemma in the most helpful way. Since you can't force a reconciliation, or control your spouse's life, being able to take control of your own life is of present, strategic importance. Your spouse knows you care; likely you have made this clear. Now to allow her or him to arrive at critical decisions apart from any pressures from you is both considerate and mature. When you come right down to it, it's the most productive approach, the most conducive to possible reconciliation.

I remember the case of an estranged couple in which the husband hounded his wife constantly. He telephoned her every day. He made excuses for going to where she was. He begged her to go to a counselor and even tried to make an appointment *for* her. He was so much in evidence that the poor wife had no opportunity to think about her feelings for him. She took it as a sign of uncaring that he couldn't leave her alone. His handling of the separation only compounded her belief that he was too dependent and immature to ever make a reliable husband.

How hard it can be for some of us to do. But it is a rule of thumb worth considering: if your spouse has left you, and has spurned counseling help from the start or after an initial session or two, give her or him more *space*—sufficient space for serious, private reflection and decision. In giving space, you evidence your caring and maturity. Sure there are times when you must contact your spouse. There are times when he or she will contact you. But if your "one last try" now becomes a hands-off strategy, it is in itself a witness to your caring and character.

Speaking of character, a counselor can help you discover and get to know better the strengths that are within you, perhaps ones that may have been awakened by this experience. You can build on these whether there is any new overture toward reconciliation from your spouse or not. At the same time, counseling can assist you in understanding as never before the subtleties of your personality, as well as the reasons why the marriage has died. It can help you accept and grow away from some of the weaknesses and dependencies.

Out of this kind of sharing, reflecting, risking, your counselor can help you see your reaction to rejection and separation as one of grief, similar to the experience of those who know separation because of death. (More about grief is discussed in Chapter 6.) Your counselor can help you get in touch with honest feelings, not only about your spouse and your marriage, but feelings of anger, hurt, loneliness, guilt, or even a sense of relief. Your counselor can guide you as you internalize forgiveness. He or she can facilitate your security in where you want to go from here. Down the line, because of your counseling sessions, you may be better prepared for the possibility of remarriage, however unthinkable that may or may not be right now.

Then add this observation: some persons are too prone to seek help. Some wear their hurts on their sleeves, ready and willing to talk with just about anyone, just about any time. They spout their troubles like a free-flowing fountain, in all directions. Or they hash and rehash, analyze and reanalyze all the happenings, whys and wherefores of the marriage demise. They wallow in the injustices of their marriage partner. It is as though they are torturing themselves, or perhaps enjoying the sympathy their story attracts.

Don't let any of that happen to you. Periodically, if need be, shut out the crisis from your mind altogether. Stubbornly refuse to let the one who has disappointed you control your life by his or her departure. Refuse to be driven to an unmanageable, horrible state of turmoil, or to feeling overly sorry for yourself. When you feel the need to talk with someone, pick a dependable friend, or a trustworthy professional person—clergyperson, family or marriage or pastoral counselor, psychologist or psychiatrist. Limit your "spreading your troubles around" to one or two confidants. You'll like yourself much better this way. So will others.

If the thought of going to a psychologist or a psychiatrist surprises or frightens you, it need not. Jokes about headshrinkers and all that may make you feel uneasy, but you need not be ashamed to consult a psychiatrist or a psychologist if you so desire. Thank God to this day for a psychiatrist who helped me at a time when I needed self-understanding most! In some ways I feel that an analyst or a psychiatrist is able to be more objective than a pastoral counselor or a minister, although I know of some of the latter who are excellent facilitators.

The crucial thing is that you find a counselor who is trustworthy. A medical man may not be necessary. There are others, including clergy types, who are trained or certified in marriage or personal counseling. As you select a counselor, seek recommendations from a friend or from someone who has found help from a specific counselor, or ask your family doctor to recommend one.

Beware of incompetent counselors! They may not be many, but it could be your unluck to find one. Beware of those who promise to restore your marriage. Watch out for those who, perhaps from religious motivation even, will act to force a reconciliation when perhaps it ought not be forced at all. For the object of any stage of marriage counseling is not to "save" the marriage at all costs; but at all costs—having given the marriage every opportunity to save itself—to work through to a solution that is the best choice for all concerned.

An initial visit and your own intuition will give some clue as to the counselor's approach and the promise of rapport and help. If you feel you are in the hands of a person you can trust, then you may want to stay with that person. On the other hand, after a few sessions, you may discover that the counselor doesn't live up to initial expectations. If so, don't hesitate to change.

One good reason for seeking out a minister, priest, or rabbi, as your preference may be, will be your previous experiences with that person, ones that make you feel you can trust the person. You likely will find a clergyperson helpful. However, there are some who dangerously may put everything in too narrow or negative a frame. Their "religion" may get in the way. They may instill more guilt than the forgiving, freeing grace and love of God.

Yes, if you have sought out professional help, or have invited your spouse to do so, hooray for that last try—that last reach for reconciliation. Regardless of the response of your spouse, keep open the possibility of returning to your counselor for your own personal growth. Remember, too, that *God* is always the faithful counselor you need.

If your sharing with the Divine Counselor is at its best, like your sharing with counselors it will not be contrived or forced. It will hold no pretentious designs on anyone, much less God. To be open, spontaneous, honest, resigning, trusting—these are your aims in prayer. Praying will help you clarify feelings and choices. It will free you to live out the crisis in your marriage with strength. It will help you grasp with heart and soul the providential hand of God that *is* able to work in all this to bring good to pass.

4
Keeping Your Perspective

DURING THIS TOUGH TIME for you, you may feel some unaccustomed pressures from within or without, so that it is sometimes difficult to keep your perspective. For one thing, *anger* may be a special problem. At times, it may have swelled and come out with frightening intensity. Knowing that the anger is there, and why you may be feeling it, will help prevent your being controlled by it.

For another thing, you may feel pressured by family or friends who are critical of the way you are handling the material side of your broken marriage. Some may want you to "push for all you can get" or may be critical because they feel you have let your spouse take unfair advantage. Putting *things* into perspective will give you greater inward security. It will enable you to keep a good balance in your dealings with your spouse, and in relation to your own material needs.

It is likely that you are feeling other pressures, too, such as those relating to the loneliness and the social and sexual needs that are part of your singled status. Also, feelings of guilt or regret may pressure from within. But I'm going to save a discussion of these for Chapters 7 and 8. Here, let's zero in on ways to keep perspective about anger and about material things.

Thank God for anger! Anger blesses. It releases pent-up fear or hurt or hatred that otherwise might be boarded up within us, destructively. If your anger should focus on your spouse, then there is nothing shameful about hearing yourself saying honestly and openly, "I hate him (her)!" If that angry you feel, then feel that angry you must. To deny that you feel thus doesn't help your emotional well-being!

On the other hand, you can't afford to allow intense anger to dominate you; and there certainly isn't anything shameful about saying, "O God, help me to forgive, and to control my anger." Bringing your anger feelings under control and into proper perspective will guard against their coming out in unexpected ways. Sometimes, as you may know, anger doesn't vent itself as outbursts of harsh feelings or words. It may, instead, lead you to do or say things you do not see as anger response at the time, but which are motivated by anger, nevertheless. Anger can lead into trite or spiteful actions or even patterns of behavior or decisions that possibly could cause you discomfort or embarrassment.

A woman of about thirty told me that, during her separation from her husband, she found herself being picky with people, particularly those closest to her. At times she was downright belligerent. Once she took her widowed, aging mother, whom she loved dearly, to a movie. While driving to the neighboring city where the movie house was located, the woman became critical of her mother's every move. During the movie, she rudely got up and went out for popcorn and drink, then came back and sat down without so much as offering her mother a thing. On the way home, the resentful attitude continued. When they arrived home, her mother said to her, with a poignancy the daughter had never known the mother capable of "Are you finished with your teenage rebellion?"

A wise mother if ever there was one! The daughter's resentment and bitterness about her impending divorce drove her back into her earlier years. She was a teenager rebelling all over again—immaturely blaming her present predicament on her parent.

Another person I know, a male of about twenty-five, became involved with another woman as an angry backlash to his hurt or rejection and to what he felt life had "dealt" him in his broken marriage. And at least one *re*marriage of my acquaintance evolved from anger motivation. Again, recognizing that anger is present helps guard against being controlled by it, in unaccustomed ways.

The anger you may feel probably springs from the hurt and disappointment you have experienced. It hurts deeply that this person you have loved and with whom you vowed to share your life "till death us do part" now has left you. If you are a parent, you may hurt for your children's sake. To suffer yourself is one thing, you may feel, but to hurt an offspring is another. Yet see Chapter 10. For children *are* tough!

I remember a young man I visited with, in his living room—after his wife had announced she was leaving him. The way he sat, the way he squeezed the can of beer in his hand, the bitterness in his voice, the way he drank in volume, made it pretty apparent that his dominant emotion was anger. I wasn't surprised to hear him sum up our visit like this: "When I think about her leaving and about the kids, it all makes me so damn mad!"

Even in some cases where husband and wife arrive at a more mutual agreement to part ways, either may feel the disappointment of a spoiled relationship. Sometimes a spouse pushing for divorce will feel this disappointment heavily. After all, husband and wife invest much of themselves in the time spent together. The energy, the effort, the caring, the pain or joy shared together, now must go the way of seeming nothingness.

Once, in the middle of an afternoon, at coffee-break time, I went by to see a friend at his place of work. I had heard his wife had recently filed for divorce. Because of the way this husband reportedly had treated his wife over the years, carelessly and loosely, I didn't expect what I found coming from my friend as we sat in the car, talking.

"We've been married ten years," he said, "and we were just getting to a point where we are out of debt and have a few things to enjoy. It all seems so—"

"Unfair!" I said.

"Right! So damn unfair. Everything we've worked for is gone now."

Yet it helps to think about that word "unfair," seriously. Think about it, please. How many times I have heard persons threatened by divorce or who have experienced it, using the word! Each time I want to ask: "Unfair by whose standards?" Usually the standards are ours, shaped by our understanding of what life or God or others appear to owe to us. Does life ever owe us *anything* really and truly worthwhile? Don't we take who we are and what we are into every experience in life and submit ourselves to the mercy of life's currents and choices? Don't we then pretty much have a say in the outcome of our venture?

Now don't interpret that as an encouragement to blame or be angry with yourself, far from it. You have done what you would do because you are who and what you are, and your partner is who and what he or she is. You and your partner—each of you—have done what might be expected of ones of your particular background and mold. It is part of the package to expect that with the gifts you have—and weaknesses—and those of your spouse,

37

life might have come to "this." Rant all day about "if only he (she) had been able to see it this way," but that will be only wishful thinking. Rant all you want about your upbringing. Be contentious about your parents, about circumstances or turn of events. Reason that with another set of givens here or there things might have been "different"—still, you don't really know that any differences would result, for sure, do you?

Again, isn't this wishful thinking, anyway? About what *is?* It may seem that with God's help and lots of growing, and a great deal of maturity, some of us may almost always stumble into situations more or less ideal. A select few may appear to almost always choose relationships that last and remain true.

But if so, it just isn't given to all of us. So believe that you've done the best you could with what you had, personally, with who you were at a particular time in history. Then begin to "write it all off as experience."

I put that phrase in quotes because it remains glued to my memory ever since spoken by a concerned friend when he first learned of my marriage collapse. The phrase was balm to my tired and angry heart. With a precise, single stroke, it helped to confirm that I had, really had, done the best I could with who and what I was; but more than that, it pointed me beyond my broken marriage to a positive promise of learning from what had happened, to growing from it. The phrase has served me well in other areas of life that have turned out to be less than expected or wanted.

The idea of "writing it all off as experience" reminds me of what Richard A. Gardner calls "W. C. Fields' Rule." One of W. C. Fields' funny but wise sayings was: "If at first you don't succeed, try, try again. If after that, you still don't succeed, forget it! Don't make a big fool of yourself!" As Richard Gardner says, "Many people refuse to learn from their mistakes." (*The Boys and Girls*

Book About Divorce, p. 152.) Gardner is writing for children, about divorced parents, but his point warms to what we are saying here. Learn from your mistakes. No use butting your head against a wall of separation that evidently is not going to give way to any stubborn, angry insistence that it do so. No use making a "big fool" of yourself by letting angry denial complicate matters for you.

Painful, angering, unfortunate in many ways all this is, perhaps; but nevertheless, your marriage death can be viewed as part of the package of life; valuable experience you must put behind you, then learn from, build from, choose from, for the future.

If even yet, with lots of professional help probably, your marriage should work out, then you can use what you have experienced in a powerful way, to mend and to mold what has been untenable and weak. If it does not work out, then angered and disappointed as you may be, it will do little good to waste further energy blaming and fuming.

Not that you should stifle your anger. Your anger needs airing, to yourself, perhaps to others, maybe even to God. But your salvation lies in refusing to be done in by your disappointment and also in refusing to hate, and learning to forgive.

As we said in Chapter 1, "the sooner you come into an attitude of forgiveness, the sooner you will be freed from the pressures of resentment." So begin now to forgive your spouse. Forgive yourself. If you do blame God, forgive God.

That latter idea may come as a surprise suggestion, but I think God understands the tendency we have to blame God when we can't blame life or ourselves. I don't think God is very quick to rap us on the head when we rave against who we understand God to be. That may be the problem, certainly, that who we understand God to be is not who God is at all. Most of all, God is not one who jumps at our every beck and call, as though God were our servant.

No, God just won't do everything you ask. Nor will God give you whatever you want or when or how you want it. God may not even be the most concerned at the moment, at least, that you have a happy home or marriage. God wants your person, committed to God. God doesn't will or want broken homes, nor yours. God *does* will happy marriages and homes for those choosing to wed. But God is great and loving enough to allow you to operate within your relationships in life as who and what you are. God is great and loving enough to allow you to make your own choices and seek your own solutions, and thus to help score your own successes or failures.

While God hasn't taken over everything for you or puppetized you, God *has* been right here with you. In your confusion, your weakness, your hurt, and yes, your anger, God has been, is present. You take it from here, now. Rebel for a time if you must. Vent your anger. To do otherwise when anger and rebellion are there could be crushing. There is plenty of divine rope for your honest feelings in God's scheme of things. But then there comes a time, or many times, when you just have to leave it all to God. Placing your hand in God's, you can take it from here in the freeing power of God for your life—whatever happens to your marriage.

ABOUT THINGS

I recall feeling pressured by some friends who were much too inquisitive about belongings I had let my spouse take with her when she left. Some also inquired about how much child support I would be paying. One friend said that I had let go of too much of my furniture.

40

Deep down inside I felt like shouting: "What difference does it make? Things, things, things! They are neither here nor there. What's here is the death of a marriage. A relationship gone kaput! A family disintegrated! Two lives shaken and being reordered!"

You probably have felt similar pressure and have felt compelled to resist it. You may have determined to be just as you and your spouse have divided or will divide material or financial assets, or liabilities. The desire to be just is commendable; so also is the spirit of holy abandon that prevents us from being driven by a lust for things. You may claim such a spirit. You may also be of a mold of character that refuses to allow enmity to temper justice in any of your dealings with others. If so, you don't want to change these qualities as you deal with the material side of your marriage crisis. You are fortunate to not have the problem of taking advantage or being revengefully greedy. Greed is self-defeating in the long run, for you, for your spouse, and for any children.

It remains, however, that you don't want to be a pushover either. Probably you cannot afford to be. You don't want to be led into reckless giving away that could make the present materially hard for you, or later be a hardship if divorce is the final outcome.

Consider the case of a divorcing person who "threw up his hands" and said, "You can have whatever you want!" only to regret it later. Possibly he acted out of a genuine desire to be fair or out of a strong sense of values. I suspect the problem could also be that at that particular point he wanted a reconciliation badly enough to cause him to lose perspective. Or he may have been too weary to fuss about details. In any case, he was unfair to himself.

So take care. Justice is fairness. It is fairness for you and yours, too, however. To settle out of desperation or without thought to your real material need is foolish and unjust. You have your own well-being to consider. Perhaps the well-being of offspring, perhaps especially if the offspring remained with you; yet even if they did not.

Still, sometimes a tearing, painful experience pushes a person toward a more lofty set of values. In that sense, you have the potential in all this for being moved *away* from a life formed from the bricks of materialism, enmity, or greed, and ever closer to one forged and solidified into something loftier. You will have profited immeasurably—while refusing carelessly to "throw up your hands"—if you are now becoming a little more convinced through all this that relationships, people, and the stuff of the spirit are of much more value than accumulations. And that love, justice, and never hatefulness, selfishness, or greed, constitute the hope of life—self-protection and all that still considered.

Not all disappointing experiences are ennobling. I'm aware of that. Witness the case of a woman who was horribly bitter all the way through separation—and finally divorce. Even five or six years later, she was trying to milk her ex-spouse for all she could get. She went on clutching and clinging not only to the past but to things and people. She was sitting on a powder keg of explosive, destructive attitudes!

Nevertheless, when you are going through the fire, there *is* a choice. You can choose to regress and solidify all your values as they are, including those you might like to see changed. Or you can reach for a loftier sense of values. You can shrivel up or you can mellow enough that some controlling devotions and some former ways of seeing things become pliable enough for change. Who knows? The child of God within you may have been waiting, dormant, for just such an experience as this fiery one, to emerge with courage!

You know it, I know it, that for some of us, it is just harder to break out and *be*. There are things we believe

42

in, we hope for, we store up and want to trust in. Somehow we go on day after day, year after year, living as though they are not. We squelch our destructive, negative emotions, too, sure—but just as surely, the positive, God-centered ones. And so it may take an experience like this to bring out into the open in a new and surprising way the person you would like to be, the person God has been pulling for you to be all along. It may turn out, in fact, that the most saving part of all this may be to look at your crisis in just this way, perhaps even be grateful for the licking of the flames.

I feel again with appreciation the honest courage in the words of a mother of two who looked back on her experience of a broken marriage and proclaimed with meaning: "It was hard, but it made me grow up, in a way I probably could never have grown otherwise. It forced me to see what really is important in life."

So your friends may be right—and wrong! You may have given too much, and haven't given thought enough to "getting what is coming to you." You may have some friends or family pressuring you to push "for all you can get." On the other hand, it may be that you have not been considerate enough of your spouse's needs. Or, you may be torn between or too torn to care. But the answer in all this is to avoid either extreme. Things *are* important, to an extent. You need them, so does your spouse. But you have felt the fiery licking. You now have touched down through the flames onto a more lasting ground of being. Your life is never going to be the same again. Things won't be enough. Necessary to survival yes, but they are not all or even most.

You are on the way to a new you. It is all being tried by fire. You can thank God for that.

5
Living
with the Legal "Mess"

THE LEGAL-LOOKING ENVELOPE chilled to the bone. I had been expecting it for some time. Resigned to its arrival, I opened it and read the summons to appear in court. I was being sued for divorce. What had been debated, pushed aside, revived again, and constantly feared, now was actually happening.

Today, at this moment, if I allow myself, I can feel again a touch of the dread that "being served with papers" brings about. Not only the dread of being served, but of the whole experience of becoming involved in litigation. The truth is that legal jargon and matters of law can scare the daylights out of some of us! The "whole mess" of legal documents, legal counseling, legal atmosphere and action, legal hearings, etc., etc., can make one feel so alone, so stripped and at the mercy of some alien process!

If separation has indeed led to divorce proceedings against you, it is my hope that you will find in this chapter some help in taking a little of the sting out of the experience for you. Here are some guidelines as you make your way through the legal mess.

1. *Select your attorney thoughtfully.* You will need an advocate, and there are many competent ones around.

Your best approach is to inquire about a prospective attorney from the divorce clients who have used his or her services. Talk with those who have used the attorney in just such a situation as you may now be involved in. Inquire from more than one client. Be sure assessments are not emotionally packed.

I know a divorced person who "blamed" a lawyer for everything, a very competent lawyer at that. The blame zeroed in on the attorney precisely because the person's divorce was granted, even though on firm grounds. I also know a person who practically made a saint out of an attorney. This for no other reason than that he couldn't reveal his mistake in choosing or his failure to switch to other counsel when needed.

Inquiring about an attorney from trusted friends or from professional persons, including possibly your minister, priest, or rabbi, could help you find one of solid character as well as competence. Or you may want to seek out an attorney you know from personal friendship to be solid.

When you have made a first-choice selection, go talk with that person. Unless you are familiar enough to feel certain about your selection, say that you want to talk without obligating yourself just yet. If this means paying a fee for consultation, it will be worth it. If you decide on the attorney visited, your initial fee will be part of the charges over the long pull. If you fear you will be disappointed, tell the attorney you "want to think about it." Or frankly say you will be looking elsewhere.

Not that you are looking for the ideal lawyer. He or she may not exist. What you want is basically two things: an advocate with whom you feel emotionally comfortable, one you can like as a person; and an advocate to whom you can respond with trust and confidence.

You do want to select a lawyer with whom you can have a basic emotional rapport. Yet even an attorney you have "liked" from the beginning may from time to time unknowingly become part of the threat of the legal process by his or her "legal manner." In fact, some attorneys say that a matter-of-fact, at times noncommittal or brief manner may be necessary to help us face up to reality when we need it. Some may feel they need to "toughen us up" occasionally. Some may take on a businesslike air at times as a protection against getting too emotionally involved. The important thing is for you to be able to feel emotional rapport and confidence in your advocate, sufficient for the long pull of your case.

2. *Ask questions.* I know a person who received a legal-jargoned letter that was far from fathomable. When he went to the attorney who wrote it with a firm statement about his inability to understand what it meant, he received a full explanation. Don't be timid! Speak your mind, ask your questions. You deserve to know what the basics of legal action on your behalf are. You deserve to understand the implications and effects of action another may be taking against you.

3. *Be open to compromise.* Know your goals and what kind of settlement you desire. Ask advice. State your convictions. At any point necessary, make clear your feelings. If need be, insist on some points you feel strongly about. But do be fair and open-minded enough to agree to reasonable concessions. You are not out, I hope, to beat or manipulate your spouse, are you? You want to protect your best interests, or those of your offspring, but you don't want to get involved in a divorce war. In the long run, being reasonable serves your best interests.

If you are in an emotional ball about the whole thing, or if you have been deeply hurt, any concession could be a severe test of your sense of fairness. If this is true, you might want to discuss where you are in your case and in your feelings with a third, trusted party. This may help you be more objective and will alleviate some of your anxiety.

You may also have questions about legal fees, and your lawyer will be glad to discuss these with you frankly.

4. *Trust your attorney to do his or her work.* If you have confidence in your lawyer, if you have selected thoughtfully, then you will be free to leave a certain amount of the work and advocacy to your attorney's discretion. That includes some decision-making. How else can your counsel hope to function on your behalf? A good lawyer consults a client at any point in the decision process—or should. Yours may not tell all, but if she or he is responsible, you will be consulted in decisions vital to the achievement of your goals. Again, if in doubt, ask. On the other hand, you may be in for a reprimand of a sort, by your counsel, if you are on the phone or in the counsel's office every other day, with queries about what is being done. That points up another suggestion.

5. *Be patient.* Legal processes take time. Court dockets are full. Legal requirements or maneuvers result in postponements. Some cases may have priority over yours on court dockets or in your attorney's caseload. There may come a time when you will want or need to push a little, or be impatient to get the whole mess over with. But meanwhile, you can settle in for the long wait if you keep in mind that waiting may be to your advantage. It may be to the advantage of your best settlement of terms. It may be that time could be what your spouse needs most to evaluate his or her options. Time can also be your opportunity for getting better in touch with your feelings and becoming more collected before your case comes up. If you and your spouse are seeing a counselor or still communicating directly, the time waiting will be needed to see what may develop from that.

6. *Keep positive your attitude toward "the law."* Some people have the feeling that law is not good. They heap negative judgments on it. They forget it is there for our protection. They forget how much, day after day, without our really being aware of it, laws shape and control our lives. The law, insofar as it protects and enhances our common and personal lives, is a gift from God. Courtrooms, documents, petitions, judges, and all the personalities and paraphernalia of the legal profession and process *can* be wearying and frightening. But thank God they are there! The whole mess is not perfect, but it is there to serve. This marriage of yours that is dying was, after all, given birth by law. The marriage may have been born of love and of God, but it was "delivered," as far as the state is concerned, by legal contract. Society has had a share in your matrimony, and society intends to have a share in its destiny.

7. *If you have children, keep them in the background.* Don't drag children into the litigation process. Keep them out of it. Not long ago a divorcing person asked me if she should take her young son into court with her. "No!" I said. "No, but no!"

In some rare cases the judge may request the opportunity to talk with children of separated parents. In some cases older children may have to be involved. But please, do not drag your young ones into the courtroom unnecessarily. No good will come of it; it will tear you and the young ones apart.

Several years ago I was asked to be a character witness for a man whose wife had sued for divorce. As I waited in the courtroom for his case to come up, a custody case was being heard. The mother of two children, about five and seven years of age, brought the two offspring into court with her. When they saw their daddy and felt the tension of the whole scene, they began to cry fearfully. There was a testimony from the mother about the father's doubtful character, all of which was heard by the children. The father then began to cry openly, too. The mother, still on the stand, was extremely cool through it all; in fact, she was so much on the flat side emotionally that I wondered about her ability to love her son and daughter. The judge finally asked her to step down and called the two children to him, behind the bench. He turned his swivel chair around, and with back to the courtroom talked with the children quietly for a few minutes. When he turned back around he sent the children back to the mother and then awarded her custody, but with liberal visiting privileges for the father. The mother became hostile and her attorney had to calm her down. Possibly, from the viewpoint of the judge and the parents at the time, it was necessary to have those children there, but what an unforgivable nightmare it appeared to be.

It will do your offspring harm, also, if you should use the litigation to downgrade the other parent before you get to the courtroom. Or if you spill your worry about an impending hearing over into your offspring's contacts with you. Refuse to allow them to be used or to use them as pawns. Even if you don't have custody of them and they are with the other parent, refuse to use them or hurt them. I repeat: if at all possible, keep your children out of it. I just can't say this too strongly.

8. *Conduct yourself becomingly in the courtroom.* If settlement of terms is finalized and agreed to in advance of the court hearing, it may not be necessary for both spouses to be present for a hearing. If you are the one being sued for divorce and you are not contesting, it may be pointless for you to go. Courts, lawyers, judges differ in what they expect, so ask your attorney about this. Be certain you are at peace with not being there. You don't want to be left with the feeling that you missed something important. You don't want to stay away just because of

your dread of the whole mess. You don't want to feel later that had you been there something better might have resulted from the hearing.

As any good attorney will tell you, you yourself are one of the most important factors in the "success" of your case. The sheer practicality of it is that it is to your advantage, if you are to be there for a hearing, to be a good witness. Be as calm and concerned and clear as possible about why you are there. Tell the truth, ordinarily answering only questions asked of you. Answer as to the point and helpfully as you can, without appearing spiteful (you're not spiteful, are you?) or biased.

Carry with you into the courtroom your concern for a fair settlement for all. If you have information or feelings to be expressed in the courtroom, by all means ask to speak with your attorney about them. But by and large you will do best to follow your attorney's lead and the directives and/or questions of the judge.

Just prior to entering the courtroom or as you enter and wait for your hearing to begin, you may experience heightened anxiety. You may be embarrassed that others you know may see you there. You may dread eye contact with your spouse. One way to lessen anxiety could be to take a trusted friend with you to court, or perhaps a close relative. Another way is to focus on the cases being heard ahead of yours. It's likely you will have that opportunity. There is a certain amount of uneasiness, in fact, resulting from so many cases being heard, in some courtrooms, and so many people being present. The positive side of it is that you can learn from experiencing what others are going through or how the judge operates. By observing the attorneys, judge, and reaction of the people, you gain some insight into what will take place when your case is called.

The above suggests something helpful you could do in

advance of the hearing date: visit your courtroom, or at least *a* courtroom, to get some feel of what a domestic hearing is like.

I recall being appalled at how many cases were being heard before the judge's bench in the metropolitan court where my divorce was granted. "Like so many cattle being led to slaughter," I remarked. I felt humiliated to have to stand (not sit) before the bench, flanked by my attorney on one side and my ex-wife-to-be and her attorney on the other. I couldn't believe it was happening like this. I had waited thirty-five minutes, stood before the judge for five more, and walked out—divorced! It was all pretty well settled beforehand, but it was an eye-opening experience. Had I visited the court before the scheduled time of my hearing, or on another day, I might have had the poise of knowing what to expect. No one, not even my lawyer, told me it would be quite like that.

Afterward, as my attorney and I stood outside the courtroom door, he said to me: "Remember now, you are no longer kin to her. Keep in touch, and let me know if you have problems." How unreal the whole scenario was—yet how gut-level real!

In my case, I felt my attorney should have told me more of what to expect, though I respect his desire not to worry me about details. I also understand that some of us suffer less anxiety and function better if we do not know all the details in advance. You can take my suggestions here in that light, fitting them to your case and temperament.

The same suggestions about being a good witness in a courtroom hearing apply to advance depositions. Depositions are used to enter facts into the record for the judge to read prior to the hearing. This saves court time; it also could mean that some of the actual anxiety of a hearing is lessened, since depositions usually are taken in attorneys' offices.

What more can we say? Dressing neatly, being punctual, courteous, helpful, while remaining conscious of your goals—these too are important when you are before a judicial bench.

9. *If you should decide to contest the divorce or any terms of settlement or custody, be very clear as to why.* This assumes that further compromise through your attorney is not likely at those points of settlement which are not acceptable to you. You will just have to sift through particular details, talk them over with your lawyer, weigh them in good faith, and make your decision as to what to accept or contest.

If you are a parent, one of your primary concerns will be with custody arrangements and support payments. Are the offspring to remain with you? If not, are you confident enough that your spouse will care for the children adequately? How able are you to care for a child? What support payments can you afford? How much support will you expect if you gain custody? What will the court expect?

Your attorney will know whether you can expect to receive, or to pay, as the case may be, a certain amount of support, or alimony in states or cases where alimony is required. Usually judges have a scale of amounts and income to use in determining acceptable support for dependents. Particular factors in each case may influence the fixing of an amount, however, so discuss these with your lawyer, frankly.

In recent years courts have been more considerate of the custody rights of fathers. If you are a father, is it possible that you can care for the children if that is your desire? You could be in for a harshly contested battle if you opt for custody, but don't write it off in the direction of the other spouse until you have thought through each child's best interests, both present and long term. I say long term because once a custody is settled, it may be difficult to get it changed. At least, you must expect that circumstances will need to alter radically enough to warrant the court's ordering a change in custody, support, visitation privileges, or other terms of an original settlement.

Some divorcing couples who are parents may want to consider joint custody. This is a plan whereby parents legally share in the control and care of the children and in decisions relating to their offspring's life. Visitation privileges, place of dwelling, etc., are mutually agreed upon. There is enough trust between the parents to believe they can work out problems that may arise, as well as operate in matters concerning their offspring with a healthy degree of flexibility. You can see how promising this could be for parents and offspring, but it takes a special kind of parents to make joint custody work. Parents need to be in control of emotions and be mature enough to keep a child's best interests at the forefront. This is why joint custody is difficult. It may not be possible or allowed in some cases. You can see why it might not work well in cases of unwanted divorce. Either spouse may not feel there is enough trust to expect that the other will carry out the spirit of the custody agreement. Very possibly, the spouse who has closed the door to reconciliation for the marriage may not even consider joint custody.

In any area for contest, you will save yourself a lot of pain, and expense, if you examine closely why you are contesting. Some persons involved in litigation may contest to be contesting. Some scream about "rights" with zeal. They drag their children into the middle of their dilemma and use them tragically, to get even. Or perhaps to maintain a hold on the spouse. The slightest concession has to be squeezed from them by their attorney. They may even bypass their attorney, ironically weakening their own case. They may be out to make the life of their spouse miserable. They are beyond being reasonable; they are scheming and void of grace.

If you resist or contest at any point, do it from a healthy perspective. Not in order to gain unfair advantage; not for ulterior motives or for revenge; not just to win a divorce war; not to please your attorney or friends or family, or some well-meaning "master mentors," as I call them in Chapter 9. If you contest, do so because you sincerely do not feel what is being put forth or asked for by your spouse is adequate or fair or best, in terms of how you see it or what you want. And what do you want? You want an outcome that is if at all possible, fulfilling for you, for your offspring, and even for your ex-spouse-to-be. You want an outcome that enhances the greatest possibility for future happiness.

10. *Throughout the entire legal process never lose your sense of personal dignity.* No matter how much the whole mess may dampen your spirits, refuse to be intimidated personally. The legal world could be completely unfamiliar to you, assuming you aren't in law yourself or haven't heretofore been involved deeply in litigation. Do not let it bring you to despair. The whole mess is a must if everyone involved is to be clear about obligations, if anything is to be decided and binding. Tolerate it for this reason, and as a means to an end, a necessity. Placing your confidence in your advocate, try to walk with an uncluttered spirit.

11. *Now hear this: place your trust in the God of grace.* And what is grace? The Bible says grace is what God is like. God is not rigid adherence to law. God is self-giving and overwhelming in loving us humans. There is nothing we can do to deserve the divine grace; there is much we have done not to merit it. But God goes on loving and accepting us. What's more, the God of grace is more interested in what is on our hearts, our grateful love for God, than in how many points we can earn or how

many laws we can keep. We please God most when we obey in response to grace, from the heart, rather than from any attempt to be "lawful" only. We please God when we go beyond what might be required, to act out of love and not out of fear.

Now to trust in a God like that, as you walk through the whole mess of the legal process, could mean some important things for you:

a. The dread you feel is lessened if God's grace is a powerful enough factor in your life to drive dread from it. In fact, being loved so freely can take the sting out of much in this world for you.

b. You will not be interested in "rights" only or in legal technicalities or demands, so much as justice and a fair settlement, a loving one. Your experience of God's grace frees you to be gracious toward others—not push-over gracious, but loving gracious. You can be open to a settlement transcending the judge's bench or "the law" only. By faith in God's grace, you are freed to work with your attorney and your spouse toward a contract that is legal, yes, but mutually upbuilding. A contract motivated by hope, forgiveness, and the grace God inspires in you.

c. You have an advocate beyond yourself who is graciously working for you and in you. The outcome of this whole mess may or may not be exactly what you hoped for. Your marriage cannot be saved, apparently, short of some miraculous turnaround by your spouse. But even this will not be too heavy for you if you walk by faith in the advocacy of God for you, believing that God is working out good and gracious purposes for your life.

If you are a Christian, you will understand God's grace to be demonstrated most of all in the love revealed to the world in Jesus the Son. The Son can be said to have taken all the mess of the world on his gracious shoulders, for us. But whatever your faith orientation, you can hold to the God of grace who will guide you and keep you strong!

6
Come to the "Funeral" and Grieve

ONE DAY DOWNTOWN I ran into a woman whose divorce was finalized that very day. With all the months of heartache and anxiety behind her, I expected her to be at least somewhat relieved, especially since she had instigated the divorce and carried through with it. She was crying profusely as we talked. Then I realized it was to be expected. She really was grieving. It was as though her husband had died, though he still lived. A "funeral" had taken place, but the body was still walking around.

To hear the words "He (she) is no longer kin to you" invites the same kind of mental and emotional response as "He (she) is dead." Only in some ways, I think, the grief of divorce is more harsh. Because your relationship has died yet still must be reckoned with in very concrete and bodily terms, it is a living death that you face. Your ex-spouse still lives. Compound that by however much your ex must be seen and related to after the divorce; your ex is like a ghost of the past constantly haunting the present.

Elisabeth Kübler-Ross's analysis of the stages of grief experienced by one who is dying, in her book *Death: The Final Stage of Growth,* is widely known now. It's almost uncanny the way they fit the experience of grief because of the separation of divorce. She speaks of five stages: *denial, anger, bargaining, depression, and acceptance.* All these stages of grief can be present in a divorced person's grief. They may have been real for you, particularly if you did not invite your separation or divorce. Yet, even when a person has sought and wanted divorce the stages may be there to a degree, as the case of the woman mentioned above illustrates.

That same case reminds me of still another. I once traveled a hundred miles or so to visit with the wife of an estranged husband, at the husband's request. She had filed for divorce, and according to him, their situation was hopeless. She "just didn't care" for him anymore, but he wanted me, as one last effort, to talk with her. I agreed, though I had never met the wife. You can imagine my surprise when I found her weeping in her concern for her husband. As it turned out, through some careful shuttling back and forth I eventually helped to effect a reconciliation that lasted until some years later— when the man was killed in an accident.

All of Kübler-Ross's stages have, in one form or another, surfaced in much of what we have shared together. Some of them can be expected to crop up again before you turn the last page of this book. Do they sound familiar to your journey through separation and divorce?

From the time of your separation, you may have denied that the death of your marriage would ever come about. In fact, you possibly denied the separation itself would ever happen, even if you were aware that your marriage was troubled. From the time of the divorce decree, you may still find yourself refusing to accept the reality of your broken marriage. All along the way, anger has stalked you often. You know what it is to bargain with your spouse, with yourself, with God, to try to coerce the outcome of things. You probably have made a few promises to life or to God if only this cup would be taken from you. Certainly depression is no stranger to you.

Thinking about bargaining as a stage of grief recalls the time I threw myself across the bed in prayerful posture. It had begun to come home to me that my marriage was threatened with extinction. I prayed: "O God, don't let it happen! Let things work out and I will do *anything* you want me to do." You have probably had similar plea sessions with life if not with God. Perhaps even to the point of being more faithful at church or in some other area of your life, as a kind of offering against the disaster to come.

Every case will be different, but depending on your actual story, you likely will experience all five of the stages. Whether the divorce decree opens up a reliving of any or all of them depends on the details of your story, and upon how much acceptance you have come to realize prior to the decree.

Even if you have had a high level of acceptance at an early point, however, the very fact of the divorce decree (the "funeral") may open up old feelings for you once more, until those feelings possibly collide with one another in painful fashion—until your acceptance is renewed again.

In a way, I think this is what happened to me. The divorce brought a reliving of all the emotions I had been through. There were depressed, saddened spirits, though mixed with some relief that it was all over. The letdown after the actual divorce was a final, necessary "churning," a last-ditch prelude to true acceptance. Perhaps it was similar to the "preparatory grief" a dying person may experience before final acceptance that he or she is soon to die—preparatory to more fully accepting the death of the marriage.

The plan in some state family codes, in providing for an initial hearing and then a waiting period, helps, from the above standpoint. The persons involved are brought before the courts, then there is a time of assessment and waiting until the divorce is declared final. Some of the grief process is stretched back into time. If and when the court grants the final decree, the effects are not so devastating, possibly.

One of the things to keep in mind is that the depth of depression that may be renewed when a divorce is granted, or how much bargaining, denying, or anger or postponement of acceptance you experience, may be unpredictable. Not only that, what may trigger a reliving of any of these is unpredictable.

Take the man who has been divorced only a month, but seems to be doing just fine. Everyone believes he has it all "under his belt." One day he shows up in my office, sits down, and breaks into tears. With sobbing voice he declares, "She called me honey." How tragic, I thought at first. They still love each other. Closer examination revealed that this might not be true for his ex-spouse. It was just that their lives had been so much a part of each other for so long that some intimacies had not died, even though the marriage had. Out of habit, the ex-spouse innocently called him what she had called him for years. No wonder it opened up feelings he thought were buried. He still loved her and was reliving his grief again.

As for tears, can't we feel free to shed them? After all, to shed tears is why God gave us tear glands. And to males as well as females. Some people cry at the drop of a hat, true. They are perhaps too emotional. But some of us are ashamed to cry at all. We think we have to be "brave and strong," even if our lives and hearts are crushed. Crying it all out relieves the heart of overflow hurting. So if in your grieving you feel like crying, go off to a place apart by yourself and cry it out. Or if you are filled to the brim with hurting and feel like crying but cannot, go share your hurt with that trusted friend or counselor. If in the process your tear glands begin to do their work, don't be ashamed. This kind of crying is OK. So are you OK when you cry. What could be more human and healing?

Now go back to the stages of grief. I find it helpful to think also in terms of a more traditional three-stage experience. Someone who loses one close to him or her through death determines to face up to what has happened, to make the best of the situation; the grieving person then may "hit bottom" emotionally; the grieving person begins to rebuild a life apart.

Now any of the three stages may vary greatly in intensity or duration from person to person. After separation from a loved one, some persons go along just fine with an outward adjustment and acceptance, in some cases even for quite some time. This is especially a possibility, it seems, when there are children or others depending on the grieving person. Being needed keeps the griever going. But eventually, almost without warning or explanation, comes the dip. The low state of mind and heart, a serious depression, brings a kind of panic, perhaps, and always great hurting. Usually this mingles with fear and anger, too. Until moving into the third stage, a person works his or her way out of the dip and upward toward a new life. There follows a more realized acceptance that he or she feels and acknowledges openly to be there.

This three-stage understanding of grief could be helpful to you as you grieve the death of your marriage. You may be able to look back, in fact, and see that after your separation from your spouse, you went through similar stages. You may find that you are experiencing one or the other now that the divorce is final. But as with the Kübler-Ross quintet, beware of putting yourself on any kind of fixed timetable, as though you can predict exactly where you are or will be at any point or in what way. You may have a fairly balanced experience: (1) "I'll make it fine." (2) "Will I ever make it?" (3) "I think I have it made now." Or, you may have a shorter time of acceptance or none at all, then experience a long, depressed time, before rebuilding. Still again, it's possible to have a short, initial adjustment but then to rebuild before that terrible low state hardly is noticed.

Knowing that such stages, such feelings often do occur in those who experience separation and divorce in a way similar to those who have lost a loved one through death tends to make for some helpful understanding. The result may be more patience with yourself; and more hope— you *will* come to the stage of rebuilding.

Patience and hope are so important. Have you sensed this as we have shared? Patience is important because you cannot hurry away your feelings. You can't hop-skip through grief or hold yourself to any series of emotions, no matter how you try. You can do some things to help you adjust, perhaps, to lighten the pain, to hasten the healing somewhat. You can share your grief with another or cry it all out, or keep faith that rebuilding will come. But in the long run, you've got to feel the pain as you alone must feel it. To try to hurry it is just more denial. It is postponement of the acceptance you must feel if you are to heal.

At the core of working through your grief, though, will be your ability to let the other go. If the death of your marriage is a fact by court decree, it follows that you must let the marriage die. You must let go of the former husband or wife as a mate, completely. Place him or her in the tomb and walk away. Not that you wish the spouse dead; slowly you may come to the point where you wish the spouse life. Chapter 12 expresses the importance of this to your own complete wholeness. You *do* need to let go, subconsciously and consciously let go.

You probably have known divorced persons who go on

for months or years after a divorce decree, refusing to release the ex. Some go on pretending they are still married to the other, divorce or not, even remarriage of the other or not. What denial! I can illustrate with the divorcé who said to me: "As far as I'm concerned we never were divorced; she's still my wife and always will be!" That kind of undying love may be admirable, but it is hardly realistic or healing. Behind it is a stubborn disregard for the feelings of the man's ex-spouse, and a disregard for the facts. The ex-spouse has made it perfectly clear there never can be a reconciliation. Even if this were not so, what about the man's disregard for himself? For clearly he has turned himself off to a measure of joy and happiness.

There is another way to look at the need to let the ex-spouse go, one relating to what I wrote about honesty in Chapter 1. Isn't there mercy for you in the knowledge, deep down inside, that the long struggle you have gone through is now past? Isn't there some deliverance, some release for you, in that? Deep within, there could be a sense of laying down a heavy burden. Your loneliness may be great, your grief may be real. But spiraling up from within all your mixed emotions there may now be a sense, if you will let it surface, that an ordeal has come to a close. Capitalize on that. Out there in the future, and starting right now, there is a hope of release from the heaviness of months, or perhaps years, gone by.

There is no selfishness in capitalizing on the release you may feel, now or later. It is a sign of strength of character, in fact, as well as the better part of wisdom, that you accept that the past is past, and that you have a future ahead of you.

One more word: you may find a new grief opening up for you if your ex-spouse should marry again before a remarriage occurs for you. For the remarriage means a final end to the end; in a sense it is another "funeral," another death you must weather. It can strike the last blow to your marriage; the final snuffing out of whatever flickering hope you may have allowed to lie dormant in the deep recesses of your subconscious. Your ex-spouse "dies," and so do you. Your loss, your rejection is complete; your separation from your former partner in matrimony is now more irrevocable.

The sorrow you may feel may be complicated by renewed anger feelings, this time possibly toward a new mate, as well as toward your ex-spouse. A new depression may set in. There could also be feelings of inadequacy or loss brought on by the thought that the ex-spouse is now "in the other's arms."

If any of this is your experience, don't lose heart. This too will pass. The wounds, though opened afresh by the other's remarriage, will heal again, in time and by faith.

If you are grieving over unwanted divorce or the remarriage of your ex-spouse, it is understandable. It's natural, to be expected. Remember, you *are* part of the race called human. Others have walked the path of grief you are walking and have emerged; most have emerged stronger persons. There is courage for you in this knowledge. As you wait and work through the genuine grief you may feel, you can emerge too. And when the fiery ordeal seems too much, at any stage or time, if you are a person of faith, ask God to help you. It's tough to get used to not being kin to someone you once loved and who loved you—someone no longer family. You may at times be tempted to declare God "no longer kin" to you, but God never is going to divorce *you*. God is the family whose comfort you need right now.

7
Receiving
and Accepting Forgiveness

No MATTER HOW BLAMELESS you may feel yourself to be in the breakdown of your marriage, you may, if you are now divorced, feel some pangs of guilt. You may feel in need of forgiveness.

Psychologists tell you that forgiveness must be realized if it is to do its healing work. By this they mean that forgiveness must be internalized. It must be more than a nod of your head. It must be acknowledged and recognized "down here" in your will and emotions, as well as "up there" in your intellect. A forgiveness gratefully received and fully accepted!

If feelings of guilt are a problem for you, here are some ideas and suggestions that may help you receive and accept forgiveness.

1. *Put the divorce decree and the fact that you are divorced in a healthy frame.* When you stood before a clergyperson or justice of the peace, and in the presence of witnesses exchanged vows with your spouse-to-be, it is likely that you meant what you said. The words "till death us do part," or "let no one put asunder," or similar words about the lastingness of marriage may, now that you are divorced, reverberate in your memory, pricking your conscience. It may be ingrained in you that *being*

divorced is wrong. But contrary to what you may think or believe others are thinking, your divorce in and of itself need not be something to feel guilty about. Even if society, or you, or others, have linked divorce to human weakness or personal wrong or failure, isn't it true that most marriages, and yes, those which appear to have succeeded as well as those which fail, may be linked to some of the same? In fact, aren't the weaknesses or possible destructive attitudes that led up to the end of the marriage of more consequence in your divorce pilgrimage than the actual fact that the marriage is now ended? Not that you are so guilty of destructive attitudes, though you may be or at least feel you are. But if so, how important to deal with *these,* as you face your feelings of guilt. Again, the divorce in itself is not the most significant thing. It marks the termination of your contract, but it wouldn't have resulted apart from all that transpired between you and your ex-spouse.

Putting the fact of the divorce in this kind of frame helps you to reduce guilt feelings about *being* divorced. It helps you to focus your mind and heart on what you *do* need to get squared away about. It opens the door to thinking about your divorce decree and about your singled status in a more positive way. Especially if you have tried to save your marriage, the divorce decree could be seen as a merciful release—a release from any further responsibility on your part for keeping it alive. Moreover, as the final stroke to your severed relationship, it marks the end of a painful experience. Then too, it opens the door to a new beginning for you—fraught with risks and uncertainties, yes, but a beginning with the potential for the kind of growth and new meaning underscored in past chapters and at a later point in this one.

At first, it may be difficult for you to view your divorce in a more positive frame. Working at it, you will build a psychological bulwark against too much guilt about just *being* divorced.

2. *If you do feel responsible for your own weaknesses that may have contributed to the demise of your marriage, consider this a sign of strength.* In fact, it's commendable if you are responsible about them, if you are penitential and broken in spirit, because you know you could have done better in many ways. Not that you should unjustifiably or morbidly blame yourself. Heaven forbid! I know a divorced person who sprinkles his remarks constantly with "I should have" or "If only I could have." He is plagued by a legion of ugly "devils" that keep raising their heads from his past no matter how many times he has dealt with them. How subtly his guilt feelings ooze their way to the surface. How poor his self-image! How strongly he needs professional counseling.

No, morbid, irrational guilt is *not* a sign of strength. What we are talking about is a healthy sense of responsibility for one's own attitudes and actions. We are talking about responsibility for those areas of your personal and married life in which you were—are—in need of more maturity and selflessness and know it. To accept responsibility for these is to be strong in spirit; it is to chalk up a mark of character for yourself. It is to evidence a measure of conscience and healthy objectivity about yourself sufficient to assure your ability to turn guilt into growth. Yet it helps to . . .

3. *Lighten the burden of guilt feelings in whatever honest way you can.* Divorce sometimes happens in spite of the best intentions. If you were motivated to keep your marriage alive and well, though it failed, then put this alongside whatever lack may haunt you. If you sought out help and tried to change your weaknesses, give yourself another plus. If you have been the victim of irreversible desertion or unfaithfulness, draw upon the pardon implied in this! Take upon you the spirit of the

divorcée who said to me: "I know I did many things wrong, things I could have done better. I know I didn't do a lot I could have to make my marriage work. But I did the best I could, and I tried so hard!"

It could also be true that *from the beginning* your marriage was on a collision course with collapse. Facing this head on can help lessen feelings of guilt. To illustrate, I can say that from the viewpoint of who my ex-spouse and I were, my own marriage may have been "licked from the start." The sum total of cradle to adulthood exposures, environment, inherent personal qualities, and inherited traits made our marriage a risky venture from the beginning. We were brought together as who and what we were. The marriage—however much we might have desired otherwise—was not going to make new creatures of us. Not in itself it was not! Like the Barbra Streisand–Robert Redford movie classic, it was a case of "the way we were." Thus I can cover a multitude of our errors by just claiming a handicapped start by somewhat ill-fitted partners in marriage.

If this is the case with your marriage, it can take a load off your heart to understand this. Perhaps you and your spouse "drifted" into the decision to marry. Perhaps you were in need of love but unable to give it to each other. Perhaps parts of the "chemistry" of personal makeup and backgrounds were not "right" for the marriage. It isn't evasion to thus put any of these things alongside your feelings of guilt. You need not be flippant about it, nor would you want to be. But you can be responsibly realistic about it. The result may be that you can bring any guilt you may feel into more actual and manageable focus.

4. *If you feel a genuine need to express regrets to your ex-spouse in any way, and the opportunity presents itself, then consider doing so.* Now if in response to this suggestion you say, "Express regrets about what?" Then

I will say, "That's up to *you.*" Perhaps you feel you do not need to speak to your ex-spouse about anything. If you were deeply offended, as could well be the case if you tried but could not save your marriage, this is understandable. Perhaps you feel that your ex-spouse, in fact, needs to express regrets to *you,* and *that's that.* Perhaps no opportunity to share with your ex-spouse promises to present itself. In any case, anything but a genuine, uncontrived, mature sharing of this kind would be worthless. Only you can judge the need or value or feasibility of it. But if you do feel it a good thing, as difficult as it might prove to be at first, it could help you, especially if your ex-spouse should respond in a positive, supportive way.

I remember a movie from "way back when," in which a young couple were divorced. Much later, the ex-wife was in a restaurant with a friend, in a different city. She may have known her ex-husband lived there, but it did not cross her mind that she might run into him. As her order was being taken, she looked up to see a familiar face—her ex-husband's! The immediate shock over, the pair began to exchange "How are you?" questions. Eventually the young man asked if he could speak to her in private. They went into the café kitchen and the young man said to his ex-wife: "I wanted to tell you that I am sorry for everything. I was so immature, in many ways. I let you down a lot. I really regret it now. But I am happy, and I wanted you to know that." He was relieved to find his confession of guilt not only accepted but countered in kind.

"It's all right," she said, "and I'm glad you are happy. I'm happy too. I was deeply hurt when you left. But I want to say how sorry I am for being so childish about some things. I thought I knew how to love you, but I guess I didn't."

Those may not have been the actual words in the

movie, but they are a good representation. They illustrate how granting forgiveness and asking for it can be cleansing for the soul. The experience is akin to what we are hearing more about these days, in regard to services of divorce or divorce ceremonies. I read recently about the minister in Dallas who offered a service of forgiveness and grace to a divorced couple, so that they could part ways with supportive feelings. Such a service might not have been possible in the case of unwanted divorce, I am aware. But the idea of clearing one's soul of barriers to guilt-free living after divorce is a wholesome one. I know of at least one major denomination that officially supports the use of such services by its ministers.

For suggestions related to expressing regrets to your offspring, if you are a parent, see the ideas expressed in Chapter 10. And how very important receiving and accepting forgiveness for yourself can be for your children and your relationship with them!

5. *Share your feelings of guilt with a reliable confidant or counselor.* They say confession is good for the soul. Is there someone whom you can trust and to whom you can bare your guilt feelings or what you understand to be the genuine shortcomings producing them? Not that you want to bare yourself carelessly. When it comes to confidants or counselors, the word is still "trustworthy," a word we cannot emphasize enough. And, in fact, you may want to seek professional help if guilt feelings are gnawing at your inward peace. The benefits you stand to experience from opening your guilt up to a *trustworthy* other are at least two: you may find, as the cause of the guilty feelings is shared, that you really are not as "guilty" as you thought; or you may discover that the prick of your guilt decidedly dulls or disappears.

A divorced woman in her forties once bared to me some of the things she had done or shared in, in the past, that were particularly guilt-producing for her. I listened attentively and quietly, humbled that she felt she could tell me these things in confidence. When she finished I was still listening, slowly nodding my head in understanding. Then I said, "It must have been hard for you to tell me these things."

Before we parted, her mood miraculously changed from one of sorrow and shame to one of great relief, almost bubbling over with every breath. She had unlocked the damnable hold of some hurts and "secrets" that had kept her slave to guilt for too long. Now she was feeling freedom at last!

A very attractive younger woman, still married, once telephoned me for an appointment. When she arrived in my office she was obviously burdened and nervous. She hesitated, then asked, "Do you think it's possible to be forgiven for hurting someone close to you?" When I answered "Yes," that I felt it certainly was possible, she asked, "Do you think I should tell my husband?"

"I don't know," I replied, "because I don't know what you've done."

"It's terrible," she said.

There was a long silence, during which she began to cry. "Would you like to tell me about it?" I asked.

"Oh, no! I couldn't! It's just too awful!"

Further conversation revealed she wasn't about to bare her secrets to me. Of course I did not push it, but I was greatly concerned that she said she could not even pray about it to the God she said she believed in. Sadly I felt she was so close to being free of her burden, yet by her insistence on keeping it inside, so far away from freedom.

Sharing your burden with another may or may not be best for you, so consider all this soberly. Surely you don't want to share in a way that will make you feel *more* guilty, or regret having shared, later. But if you choose your confidant or counselor with care, acceptance rather than condemnation is likely. The result could be release and recharging of spirit.

6. *Remember that you cannot force or earn forgiveness.* A man with barely twoscore years behind him nevertheless managed to fill those years with some attitudes and actions that bothered him very much. One day, as we talked over coffee, he asked, "What do I have to do to be forgiven for some of the things I have done wrong?" I hadn't heard the question quite that way in a while, so I thought before answering. Then I said, "Nothing. Absolutely nothing!"

I backed up a little to qualify that as we talked—about possible ways to make amends. Still, the ultimate answer is that you cannot *earn* forgiveness. Nor can you force it! Freedom from guilt feelings can be realized; forgiveness will come, but not by making points with yourself or anyone else, or even God, if you are a person of faith. Nor will it come by some act of will alone. So our seventh suggestion is so very important.

7. *Receive and accept forgiveness, as a gift.* By "receive" I mean open yourself to forgiveness (and do not try to force or earn it). By "accept" I mean let forgiveness permeate your soul, just believe it and let it *be*. In the same vein as W. C. Fields' Rule referred to in Chapter 4, when you have put your divorce decree in a proper frame, when you have responsibly faced up to your actual weaknesses, when you have lightened the burden of guilt feelings in whatever honest ways you can, when you have considered saying or have said you are sorry as the need or opportunity is there, when you have aired your feelings and shortcomings with a trustworthy confidant or counselor, then *forget it!*—forget your guilt as much as is humanly possible and *believe* forgiveness. Receive it and thus accept it, as a cleansing, freeing gift!

Not so easy as it sounds, of course—receiving and accepting forgiveness as a *gift*. It's sort of like the

71

experience we had in our family recently. My wife came home from the grocery store to find two men installing a beautiful console color television set in our den. All we could learn is that "some friends" had given it. Another friend said, as I told her about the marvelous surprise, "It shows somebody likes you." She was right: it *was* self-affirming. And we were deeply grateful. Yet it took several days for us to *really* receive the gift. We couldn't thank the people personally, not knowing who they were; the enormity of their thoughtfulness was overwhelming; our inability to ever repay them, humbling.

How hard to receive the marvelous gift of forgiveness too! It may take time to move from receiving to truly accepting. It can be humbling. It can be self-affirming too. It can move you to gratitude of the deepest sort. But who gives the gift of forgiveness?

8. *Take your need for forgiveness to God.* I suppose it is possible to receive forgiveness from Life. I *know* you can experience it and receive it from another person. But if you are a person of faith, the giver of forgiveness is not anonymous to you. You take your guilt before God. You believe that receiving forgiveness at all traces back to God. If confession is good for the soul, as a person of faith you can know the soul-refreshment of confessing to God those ways you may have "missed the mark" in marriage or in any relationship or area of life. That, by the way, is what the word "sin" means—to "miss the mark."

You see, the Biblical understanding of God compels our belief that the divine forgiver has no desire to withhold from any person the gift of forgiveness. To carry a burden of guilt when God wants to carry it for you is to be in need of counseling; it is to refuse to believe that somebody divine likes you. It is to beat yourself on the back for nothing. It is to enjoy stifling new life God wants to draw from you by means of every experience. It is, tragically, to play games with good news.

On the other hand, to receive and accept the cleansing, freeing forgiveness of God into your whole person is to reflect the fully good and whole and loving God! It is to confess that God truly is a God of love. God isn't fooling. Why won't you and I believe divine forgiveness? Why can't we forgive ourselves if God does just that?

Those of Christian persuasion see the good news about forgiveness demonstrated in the self-giving love of God poured out on the cross of Jesus. The wretchedness in us, our "missing the mark," is felt, admitted within us, and the cross shows us God doesn't condemn us.

If you are not a Christian, you may believe in the God of self-giving love. Your good news is also that we are accepted though we are undeserving and broken.

What God wants us to do is to open to and embrace divine acceptance of us. Then to go on living free and forgiven, healed and whole.

9. *Forgiven, you are free to grow.* It is almost too good to be true, really. In fact, I remember well the change in my thinking from guilt to growth. Actually, I felt uneasy that I might be taking my broken marriage too lightly if I moved beyond it to greater wholeness because of it. That uneasiness was a kind of residue guilt, I now see. I see that to internalize forgiveness and turn marriage failure to growth is not to devalue marriage itself or one's marriage commitment of the past. In fact, if people ask me now if I believe in divorce, they are likely, if they know I have been divorced, to back off a minute and ponder my answer. For I will say, "No, I do not." My "No" is an affirmation of my belief in marriage as a lasting commitment between two persons, which I see as the divine intention. Yet the gift of forgiveness means I was and am free to seek wholeness and joy. In my case this has included the joy of a second, lasting marriage as well.

And my "No" answer sometimes has to share a little

space with a realistic and compassionate "Yes" too. "No—but yes I believe in divorce." The yes part because I understand that divorce *is* a reality, *can* be a necessity or a merciful solution or the lesser of two evils, and at times *is* unavoidable. I also believe that a person can *grow* from divorce; divorce, if it must be, can result in positive growth.

No doubt the death of your marriage pains the divine heart. But I believe that even more important to God than the success of your marriage has been all along your potential success of the spirit. That belief was put like this in Chapter 4: "God wants your person, committed to God." This is why God will use your broken marriage to help you grow, why you are now free to grow from your experience. The possibility for meaning and wholeness becomes promising beyond your broken marriage, as you receive and accept the gift of forgiveness from the loving God.

I know. You feel like a statistic. You *are* a statistic. But be a redeemed one. You will spark admiration and hope in others by your having come through the fire a forgiven, renewed-in-the-spirit, and free-to-grow you!

8
Living
with the Loneliness

IS IT ANY WONDER if you are lonely? Going from coupled to singled tears and wounds. It pulls you apart from another who has been a significant part of your life at an intimate though conflict-producing level. Like a severed limb of your body, the partner in marriage no longer is "there," yet bequeaths a lingering sense of being there anyway.

Especially if you must circulate in the surroundings of home, work, community, or play, where the absent partner once circulated with you, loneliness is inevitable. Wherever you go, the lingering memories of the other will not be far away—that familiar place in the yard or kitchen where he or she always stood; the seat beside you in the car; the other half of your bed; the echo of the voice once filling a favorite room of the house; belongings left behind; a place of employment; that certain restaurant you frequented together; a park where the two of you jogged or took walks.

You may honestly be relieved that the conflicts of your marriage have come to a halt in your life. You may no longer circulate where your partner once circulated with you. But a psychological void lingers. The loneliness you feel is one of *being torn emotionally*, of not being complete as before.

Part of this incompleteness may relate to the sexual intimacy of marriage. The final section of this chapter is written to help you face your sexual needs.

The loneliness you may feel could be one of *being altered,* also. To change your life-style by design, or by gradual evolution in the ebb and flow of life, that is one thing. To have your life-style complicated by the decision of a spouse to leave you—that's quite another. The result is added responsibilities and a solo pattern of living now imposed on you.

Once when I commented to a friend of mine that he must be feeling the pressures of having to live alone, after his wife had left him, he replied with surprising belligerence: "I don't like it!" He wasn't positive anymore that the marriage would work if his wife should return; yet he felt keenly the alterations in pattern of living that her departure brought him. As we talked, I realized that he felt the loneliness of doing more things solo. What he had shared with another, or left to another to do for him, now was totally on his shoulders. There was a shift in load as well as a shift in responsibility. He had no children; but the tasks of daily living, including cleaning house, caring for the yard, paying all the bills, answering the phone, doing laundry, cooking, now were his *alone* to do.

You can duplicate this singled person's feelings a thousand times from the particulars of the life world you and your spouse shared in together. For example, if you have children, and they are with you, you may feel keenly your altered life-style as you share in the active beginning of a new day, preparing for and eating breakfast as a family, or in getting the children dressed for school. You must now go it alone in the routine of doctoring hurts, in getting the kids to piano lessons or Scout meetings, in the routine of tucking in, etc.

76

You may or may not have been an independent person. All of a sudden now you must make decisions; you must carry responsibility for all if not most of it; you must go it alone. There may be shared responsibilities or decision-making in some areas, of necessity, for a divorced couple—even if they live some distance from each other—but there are bound to be a number of areas where you just have to risk it alone, and bravely.

Some homemakers particularly, who have not worked outside the home, may not have prepared themselves for assuming full responsibility for some areas of their life. They not only are not used to making solo decisions about the rearing of offspring or about other family matters, they find it new to express more than a passive interest in financial or business affairs. When separation or divorce comes, they soon discover how independent they need to be. They realize they have lost not only a spouse but a helper, if not a breadwinner; a co-worker, if not a staff to lean upon. It's a lonely walk.

Separation or divorce produces loneliness in another way too. Much of what was *enjoyed together* now is done alone. For one man I know, the joy of watching a football game on television, which in the past he thought he cherished doing alone, now brings unrest. He used to call out his exuberance after the big play by his favorite team. It just isn't the same without his wife in the next room to hear or to poke fun at him. Besides, he misses the niceties of having his wife bring a drink as he sprawled in the recliner or having her sitting down for a moment to watch with him. Now he has to get the drink for himself or forgo it. He would gladly have given up those football games to have his wife back, though.

Or take the case of a woman who enjoys working in the yard *with* her husband. Probably the best communication between them is at such times, although it is mostly nonverbal. Then comes divorce—and the woman loses interest in yard work.

Social situations and connections also may generate loneliness for you. Whereas the two of you used to go out together, or with other couples, now you may have to go it alone, or at least alone with others. Whereas you used to relate to people of the opposite sex as a person committed to another, now you must relate unattached. If you aren't certain just how dead and over your commitment to your ex-spouse is at this point, you may feel awfully lonely as you relate in limbo.

You may have played tennis or golf with your marriage partner, or gone to the same clubs or friends' homes together, or attended the same places of worship together. Now these activities or places bring a special kind of awkwardness, and yes, a new brand of social responsibility. If your former spouse lives in the same vicinity and continues to show up in similar places, there may be added loneliness. Never more than in social situations does a separated or divorced person feel keenly that he or she walks alone.

Heightening the sense of being lonely because of social awkwardness will be the difficulty of your well-meaning friends to understand what you are feeling. They may assume it simple to take up where you left off, without your marriage partner. They may take for granted that you will frequent the same old haunts and social circles as before dissolution of your marriage. They may think taking hold of added responsibilities is a snap. They may not realize how much your life-style has been altered or how it all relates to what you are feeling inside.

I recall being invited to share in a meal at the home of some old friends, after my divorce. How like a misplaced prop in a stage setting I felt! Granted that the feeling of not being in place was mostly within me, I can recall the loneliness made stronger by a desire not to impose or to be treated like a special case.

Special? Well, what about the *stigma* attached to divorce? Can it add, in itself, to loneliness? It depends on how you view your new status as a divorced person. Going from coupled to singled carries a label; there's no doubt about that. You don't have to put on an "I'm divorced" tag. Others can read the situation. You know they know things are different with you. Your loneliness is one of dying inside because you must now walk before others as one who erred or has been erred against. In this sense, I could carry our discussion back to Chapter 2. Yet I mean more than loneliness deriving from a blow to your ego. I mean a loneliness born of the stigma of divorce. You are lifted out of one category (married) and into another (divorced). You're a statistic; you represent an altered institution; a home broken; a legal contract nullified; a union divided. If you remarry one day, you may discover that your label follows you. You will then be a divorced person who has remarried!

I haven't said anything about *rejection* as a part of loneliness. It needs to be said. Being rejected by your partner in marriage is, in itself, enough to create a special kind of loneliness. Especially, perhaps, if you have been rejected for another! Not to be loved anymore by someone you have loved, perhaps still care about, cuts and wounds. It's a lonely kind of wound, because only you can feel it as you do.

Ways to Cope with Loneliness

How do you deal with the loneliness, whatever reasons generate it? I share these techniques and attitudes.

1. *Accentuate the positive side of the aloneness.* You didn't ask for the loneliness, but is there value in the *aloneness?* Television programs that you *alone* want to

watch, activities or hobbies that you *alone* would like to enter into. Books you haven't had time to read—can they now be given more of your total attention? Aren't you now getting in more solo time with your child or children? True, your responsibilities, if you are a parent, may now be greater, but the time you spend with that son or daughter is bound to be more one-to-one, isn't it? So isn't there a *healthy* side to your relationship to them?

And if you don't have custody of your children, the time you do spend with them may be more in-depth. Not only that, you can be grateful for some absence of conflict for them. Can't you recall, possibly, times when they ended up in the middle, left with all the emotional insecurity which that implies? You and your spouse may have disagreed concerning their discipline or other matters important to their lives. You miss them, very likely, but the loneliness is softened by the hope that perhaps their lives are made a little less complicated and more tranquil.

Actually, all of this is making your loneliness work for you as a blessing in disguise, the same technique pointed up in Chapter 1. That technique will be one of your greatest allies in coping with loneliness.

2. *Seek out the companionship of others when you are lonely.* When being alone gets heavy, reach out to others. When you are feeling desperately alone, call a friend for a visit, a game of tennis, a round of golf, a cup of coffee, a shopping trip. Participate in the life of your church or synagogue or other support group, in spite of the loneliness of going it alone. Refuse to live in a shell.

3. *Accept the hospitality and companionship offered by others, but be brief and discreet.* How pathetic the divorced person who stays and stays and stays, until asked to go home so the hosts can go to bed! Or what a nuisance the singled person who comes around at mealtime and doesn't have enough social grace to say no to a

dinner invitation, at least some of the time. Or how overbearing the person who overdoes the golf or tennis bit by always pushing for a partner.

4. *Feel free to say no.* When you don't want to be in a situation that puts a strain on you, or when you feel uncomfortable about socializing, feel free to decline. There are those who, because they are concerned about you, may overdo *their* reaching out. They should understand if you say simply, "Really, I don't feel much like it this time." To say no is your right and privilege when it comes to matchmakers, too, as I suggest in Chapter 9.

5. *When you feel overburdened, give yourself breathing room.* You may need space if unaccustomed or heavy responsibilities weigh you down. Do you have to be a perfectionist in housecleaning, in yard work, or in some details of work or business? Can you afford to get some paid help to lighten the load? Do what you enjoy, what you have time or inclination to do for a while, what you must get done; then leave the rest to a better day. Sure, all of this within propriety and good sense; but don't let yourself get overpressured at any one time, that's the point. Or allow your loneliness to cause you to lose yourself in work and worry so completely that you create more loneliness!

6. *Seek advice from a trusted friend or knowledgeable confidant on decisions that threaten.* The loneliness of decision-making is greatly lessened when you feel that you have, at least, considered the angles. You don't have to follow the advice of just any "master mentor," or even the advice of a trusted close friend or other person. You will make a more knowledgeable, less lonely decision if you share the load of decision-making a little.

7. *Remember that you are your best friend—or your worst enemy.* Sulk in your loneliness if you wish, but at your own peril. Reach out in your loneliness if you can, and to your own growth. By taking an attitude of strength

and refusing to lick your wounds indefinitely, by mustering some of that acceptance and honesty and faith we wrote about in Chapter 1, you are freeing yourself to overcome loneliness.

8. *Affirm that God loves you.* Having been rejected by your wife or husband, this is good news you need. God has far more reason to reject you and has not. God loves you. That may seem trite on signboards or bumpers, but now it is pretty dynamic theology. Nothing will ever separate you from God's love. God is intentionally with you because of divine love for you. Believing this will help you walk through the loneliness of familiar haunts, of rejection, of feeling stigmatized or overburdened because of altered life-style or weighty decisions. It will help because you will have a sense of having your hand grasped firmly by Another. There is security and stability in that.

I can recall being steadied by the knowledge that there were those close enough to my situation who were remembering me not only by gestures of friendship or family support but by their praying. How it helps to know that others are walking with you, through their prayers.

FACING YOUR SEXUAL NEEDS

In one of the Motley's Crew comic strips, Mike asks Earl about Earl's attempts at "picking up girls." Earl admits his shame. Then a girl walks by and Earl says, "Look at *that* babe!" as he jumps up to follow her. Says Mike: "I thought you were ashamed?" To which Earl responds: "I am . . . I'm gonna try for deep regret!"

A point worth considering! There are some acts and involvements that can embarrass us before others because they are contrary to our sense of what is right or wrong or acceptable for us or for others. Then there are some acts and involvements that more than embarrass;

they bring on enough misery to cause us deep regret.

When we talk about sexual needs of separated or divorced persons, the friendly two-pronged warning is: take care not to fall into shame; take more care not to fall into deep regret.

Consider these ideas:

1. *If as a separated or divorced person you should feel pressured toward sexual fulfillment, this is understandable and normal.* After all, a pattern of sexual intimacy, fulfillment, and release has been established over the months or years you have been married. It has been a part of your life. It has involved more than your physical makeup. It has involved you psychologically and emotionally. Depending on how much of a love relationship you had and how meaningful your sex life has been, it has involved you perhaps spiritually. It stands to reason and reality that because this sexual pattern has been broken by separation and divorce, you could be deeply affected. There is a block to fulfillment and release that is physical but more than physical; a shift in your pattern of life; an adjustment of your whole person. Need you be surprised if difficulties are encountered, drives felt deeply, and loneliness endured? All of that adds up to a special kind of pressure, but all of it is normal.

2. *Some feelings can deceive you.* Feelings of guilt, for example, can lead to later-to-be-regretted involvements. In effect, the involvements provide the punishment for guilt which the person feels he or she deserves. Loneliness can lead to involvements or complications that appear to be satisfying but that can bring regret and more loneliness. They are not lasting or personal enough to absolve the loneliness. Anger because of what has happened or a desire to hurt the person departed can push one into temporary fulfillment; self-pity with an "I don't care anymore" kind of feeling can do the same.

I have seen some divorced persons take on a "what the

hell" attitude, which, being interpreted, means: "I have failed in marriage and so I might as well mess things up by having an affair also." Not that the person verbalizes all this; usually the rationale for the affair is arrived at unconsciously.

The antidote to being tricked by your feelings? Insofar as possible, face them honestly, accept your divorce openly, get in control of your feelings and thus your actions.

3. *Know who you are sexually.* That means, know how you feel about sex and know what you feel about your own identity as a sexual being. To be a healthy sexual being, a man or a woman, is to know that sex is good and to appreciate that you are sexual. In the case of separated or divorced persons, it is to know also what kinds of sexual fulfillment do or do not bring true reward. It is to be able to set one's limits with confidence and to feel comfortable in living within them. It is to know what will bring you into shame or regret. It takes a maturing person to put one's actions in tune with what is acceptable or unacceptable, so that conflicts and complications do not result.

Some divorced persons, by the way, apparently feel no pangs of conscience about having sex relations occasionally with the person divorced. Sometimes this very thing happens without deliberate planning. A kind of flashback happening is set up by lingering feelings of attachment, which may or may not involve genuine caring. You need to be aware of the heartache that may be brought into your life by sexual reinvolvement. If you have been on the road to acceptance of your separated state and then are drawn back into a close, even though overnight-only experience with the ex-spouse, it could open up some hurts. It may build some hopes that might set you back in your adjustment for quite some time.

By the same token, beware of being fooled by the hope

that if you can sexually get your former marriage partner back into bed with you, love will return and all will be well. The great chances are that this is wishful thinking, at best. It is wishful thinking unless there are other signs that a new relationship can be rebuilt on more lasting foundations than sexual attraction only. Besides, it is possible you will just go deeper into loneliness, frustration, feelings of rejection or guilt, and only add to your burdens.

4. *You don't need any new burdens.* You have and will have enough loads to carry as you continue working through your separation and divorce. The burdens of guilt feelings, of deep regret, of flippant relationships or halfhearted obligations, you need "like a hole in the head." And what about burdens that go beyond feelings and obligations to more serious problems—the dangers of venereal disease, or unwanted pregnancy, or other complications that might arise from hasty decisions? That isn't to say that you would allow this kind of thing to happen; it is to acknowledge that it does happen to some people.

5. *Try sublimating your sexual drive.* That may sound old-fashioned, but the energy you ordinarily would channel into a sexual relationship can be directed to other fulfilling pursuits. Whether it be through a new beginning in a sport that has interested you, through the development of some hobby or artistic talent, through service to others or giving yourself to a larger cause, through a new challenge in your work, it's possible to sublimate your sexual drives in a meaningful way. Sublimation will give some of the release you might have found in marital sex. I know this to be possible because within marriage itself it happens. There are times and seasons when either partner is so involved in something that demands his or her whole person, that sexual drive spends into the absorbing pursuit. It could work for you, too, now.

6. *Beware of the cop-out, "Who will know?"* We have come full circle with this. The fact is, even if you feel you can become involved in extramarital sexual relationships without deep regret of heart, mind, body, or soul, you still need to face the possibility of shame, of social embarrassment. What *will* your family or friends think? Their opinions of you may be important to you. And if others do not know and you don't have problems knowing yourself, then there is the faith-fact that God knows.

If you are a person of faith, it comes down to this: you want to be able to live with yourself before God. Your faith can help you know your sexual limits and who and where you are sexually. It will help prepare you if temptation comes. It will help you, as a sexual being, to maintain meaningful relationships that do not invite shame or regret.

Let this young divorcée sum up the loneliness of separation and divorce for us: "I feel like climbing the walls. Today, I tried to cook but ended up boiling water for one of those frozen food bags. I have grown tired of eating out. It is damn lonely. Suddenly being alone, one realizes how much of the past has been filled with sights and sounds—and how meaningless much of it has been. It is a period of my life in which the past has been closed and the future is so uncertain." (Reported by Richard Lyon Morgan, "Divorce: Forgivable in Clergy?" *Presbyterian Survey Magazine,* March 1982, p. 22.)

Scary the path beyond a broken marriage! But with faith as your guide and the assurance of God's love in your heart, you never will walk it alone.

9
How to Deal with Master Mentors and Matchmakers

MY FIRST PLAN was to write two separate chapters, one on matchmakers and one on what I call "master mentors." The chapter on matchmakers would have appeared here, the other some chapters back. I decided the two types have enough in common, however, to call for a similar strategy in dealing with them. Both are trying to be helpful; both may be family or friends; both can be misguided; both sometimes are overbearing, however well-intentioned; both can be said to be playing games with people.

The matchmaker, who is playing the love and companionship game, reasons: "What a shame for such and such to be alone!" Solution: Nullify such and such's singleness. The matchmaker may have a friend or relative who appears to be "just the perfect match" for the separated or divorced person. That friend or relative may also be separated or divorced, though not necessarily.

The master mentor plays the advice game. This master at giving advice and offering guidance, like the matchmaker, may not have any malicious intent to dominate or control. But there is a carelessness about the advice given at times that could invite a charge of cruelty.

Two key experiences will illustrate. The first reflects

both mentor and matchmaking mentality. Get the setting: I am talking with a relative. I share mixed emotions about my divorce, my hurt. I expect him to at least listen, to understand. Abruptly he asks, "Is your divorce final?" Not how long ago or how did I feel about it, but is the thing over and done with? When I reply that the divorce is final, he then inquires, "Have you met anyone you're interested in?" When I say that I may have, he just says, "Then marry her!"

Just like that! With all the insensitivity and uncaring pragmatism I would least have expected from him.

Another experience reflects matchmaking mentality. I am having Sunday lunch in the lovely country home of some older friends. I have arrived totally unknowing that their unmarried daughter will be present. After a pleasant enough meal and a visit I am asked to give the daughter a ride home. I agree, of course, but as superficial as our conversation has been during the ride back to town, I am highly appreciative of her honesty as I let her off.

"Thanks for the ride," she says. "Let me apologize for my parents, though. They're worried that I'm not yet married. To be married is heaven to them. They expect it to be so for me. They also are much aware you're recently unattached. But they mean well, and I hope you'll forgive them for matchmaking."

Her remarks inspire my first suggestion about how to deal with matchmakers or would-be master mentors: *Assume they mean well.*

You may yet be or already have been the target of the matchmaker:

"Why don't you let me get you a date with my sister's cousin or my neighbor's brother (etc., etc.)?"

"Oh, I didn't tell you Sue was coming over tonight! Sue, this is . . ."

"Tom just happened to drop into town today, so I invited him over, too."

And you have or you will collect a stockpile of uninvited advice:

"Are you going to let her keep the TV and the car? Well, if I were you . . ."

"Why, you can't let her have the baby!"

"If I were you, I'd push for all the child support I could get!"

"Good riddance, I say. You're too good for that ——, anyway!"

"If I were you, I'd go see Brother Fixit. He'll pray for you!"

Ad infinitum!

Yet, these master mentors and matchmakers may care enough to be there. Some may be malicious meddlers, I suppose, but most are not. They probably want to help. They are saying: You matter to us. You belong. They care enough to want to help with advice, however ill conceived in some instances. They hope to erase your problems of loneliness by setting up a new romance. They are forgivable when you look at their efforts in this light.

On the other hand—and here's the pitch that brings your appreciation of their caring into balance: *Keep your guard up!* As you relate to either type, don't be taken in too easily.

Advice is cheap. It can be dangerous and deceptive. We go back to what we said about counseling in Chapter 3: if you need advice, "the crucial thing is that you find a counselor who is trustworthy." Trustworthiness means that advice is given sparingly; support and acceptance are offered freely, lovingly.

Matchmaking also can be dangerous. Just as deceptive, too. If you are vulnerable because of loneliness or have not yet worked through to sufficient acceptance of your dilemma, you would do particularly well to keep your guard up. And . . . *learn to say no!*

To say no is your right. More than that, it is your obligation to yourself. If you are so inclined, say no to the would-be mentor. You are the judge of whether her or his advice is trustworthy. You may need the guidance of a *trustworthy* counselor as you think through alternatives, but in the end, you have the right to put the brakes on advice or pressures from others.

You also owe it to yourself to unapologetically say no to any overtures to a new relationship set up by others, just as you have the right to say no to any social invitation, as we pointed out in the preceding chapter. You may or may not be ready for a new relationship at this point in your broken union. If not, any arrangement made without your complete knowledge and consent is an abuse of your dignity.

I say this fully knowing that you could be put in touch tomorrow with the most marvelous angel that ever walked into your life; you could end up living happily ever after, providing you are so inclined to get involved. But no one has the right to force a contact for you. Asking your consent or at least letting you know that an introduction to an "unattached party" may be in the offing is a small courtesy. The word to matchmakers is: Be open, honest, straightforward about intentions. Respect the right of the friend or relative to say: "No, thank you. Not just yet! Someday maybe, under other circumstances, when there are more clear and certain feelings. But, no, not now."

If you do find yourself in a setup situation, you are free—as the woman I told you about above was free—to be honest—to say no.

So it comes to this also: *Be your own person.* The sooner the better! Ideally, from the beginning of your marital crisis, but at every point, cultivate the kind of responsible approach that says: "I am trying to be in control. I may not know all the answers, but I am trying to be in touch with true feelings, and I accept where I am at this point. I don't understand everything about where I've been or where I'm going, but I have some idea of where I am. I'm free enough to say yes—or no.''

Your chances of being your own person are enhanced if you are *seeking to be God's person.* For faith opens up the resources and advice of God; even better, it opens to a relationship beyond yourself that will, indeed, strengthen your resolve and hold you steady and set you free. As you walk the gauntlet of decisions and encounters that are inevitable, faith matches you with the one and only Master Mentor. Faith also enables you to hold those well-intentioned helpers up—or off, as the need may be—in prayer.

10
Children Are Tough!

LABEL THIS CHAPTER for parents, but *not* for parents only!

If you have no children, I hope you will read this chapter anyway. It will help you understand what divorced parents are going through. We would say we could not conceive of our lives without having had and known our children. We love them. However, we do wish many times that we could have spared them some of the pain. Oh, how desperately we wish that! Our wishing is the measure of our love for them.

Wishing that, because of our love we refuse to be burdened down with guilt about them. In fact, we take any guilt relating to them before the throne of grace right quickly. To do less is fraught with dangers for our offspring. The risk of spilling over onto them is too great and too costly. A positive, liberated attitude toward ourselves will mean for our children a much better chance at coming through unscathed emotionally—and for us it will mean greater peace.

More about this in a moment, but first let me counsel: if you do have a child, or more than one, trust each one to walk *with* you.

I'm convinced some divorced parents stiff-arm their

children emotionally. They hold them at a safe distance so they can't feel the young ones' hurt. They hide their own hurting. It's less painful that way, for the moment at least. Less painful, but sad, isn't it?

Not that you want to burden your offspring too greatly. You don't want to stir up their guilt or encourage them to wallow in self-pity. But for their own healing and yours, you can let them into your hurt gently, as you open yourself to their own. It's healthier that way.

The most opportune time to establish a mutually supportive relationship is from the very beginning. Explaining separation or divorce to children is no picnic, I'll grant you. But done simply and appropriately, it can make a healing difference. For one who has not wanted separation or divorce, the challenge is hard.

For separation, it could go something like this:

"Daddy (Mother) is gone now. We haven't been too happy together so he (she) chose to get away, at least for a while. Like you, I wish he (she) hadn't moved away. It hurts me that this is happening, just as it hurts you. We'll both be hurting about it together at times, but we'll be brave, too, and make the best of things. And remember, it isn't your fault that he (she) left. He (she) still loves you, and having you with me means a lot to me because I love you, too. If we help each other, we'll be OK."

Or: if the children are not to be in your care, take the same positive approach, hard as it is. Change the details to fit. Ideally, you and your spouse and the offspring could sit down and share together, whoever is caring for the children. This may not be possible, though, and you don't want to try it unless you're sure it will be a harmonious experience.

If divorce is final, try something like:

"Daddy (Mother) and I have been living apart since he (she) left, as you know. Well, he (she) has decided that we will all be happier if we are not married anymore.

We'll all go on trying to be happy, apart from each other. You'll stay with me, and Daddy (Mother) will live in his (her) place. We still will see each other, though, and we both love you. This isn't your fault and you are not to feel you are to blame in any way. Any questions?"

An older child will require more answers and will have more questions, perhaps. Here also keep it uplifting, honest. You need not shoulder blame where blame is not yours. You can be open about honest hurting and about the fact that you wish things were otherwise. Some things you may tell; some you save till later, perhaps even years, to tell. Some you leave to your spouse to share. Some things you never tell!

You're not infallible, and you just have to risk "mistakes." Care in sharing, as you follow your own good intuitions and knowledge of your particular offspring, will give their well-being the priority it deserves.

A child of separated or divorced parents will have her or his well-being best served if either parent refrains from degrading the other in the child's presence. That's hard to do when you have strong feelings, or when the other person's words or actions might not be what you feel they need to be. It's hard to save frank discussions for private times with the other parent. But do otherwise and it can be woe betide for your son or daughter!

How horrible this incident, shared with me by a divorced mother. With her three children playing in the same room, she got into a knockdown, drag-out fight with her recently remarried ex-husband, over the phone. Instead of sending the kids from the room, at first she tried to talk softly and with careful choice of words. Before she knew it came the explosion! She screamed into the phone from the bottom of her lungs. Finally, she called the oldest boy, about ten years of age, over to the phone and said, "Will you tell this bitching daddy that we don't need his interference in our lives anymore?"

The boy took the phone and I have no trouble imagining the pain in his face as the father asked him if he wanted to come live with him. The mother got wind of this and took the phone and abruptly hung up.

If your ex-spouse marries again, you may find yourself battling new emotions that could also be hard for you to keep in tow. Another dimension now enters the picture— stepparent relationships. Younger children may begin to speak of "my other daddy" or "my other mother." Or to talk of things the stepparent has done, some of which you may not approve, which may anger or threaten. You may not like the role a stepparent plays in your child's discipline and nurture. The green-eyed monster, jealousy, may surface, as you wonder if you are being replaced as a parent.

If you should remarry, similar feelings and concerns may stir within your ex-spouse, in regard to your new wife or husband. Again, the key will be to spare the child, if possible, while trying to resolve differences with the best interests of your child at heart.

It is possible a lot of children would adjust to stepparents a great deal quicker if we parents would trust them. A divorced father who married a second time related the trauma of introducing his new wife to his son of four years of age. "This is Liz, my new wife," he said to the son. He was both relieved and amazed as his little boy responded warmly with a big smile, "Are you my mother too?"

Your children may have more resources than you think for coming through when needed in stepparent relationships. If only we adults would take their trust at face value and not adulterate it by our petty jealousy or concerns.

Actually, how to be a good stepparent has got to be a

subject for another book. What we're saying here is that control and caring by stepparents, by you, and by your ex-spouse can go a long way. With enough concern for the well-being of the offspring and for all of you, things may not get all that entangled. That may sound idealistic, but it's worth working for. And if you don't have the cooperation of the other adults involved, it's worth the effort you put in on your own. Your concerned, mature approach may be just what is needed to inspire others— just the spark of life to prevent serious damage to your offspring, over the long pull.

A word here about attitudes toward child support: whether you are the one paying support or receiving the payments and using them in trust, it adds to the quality of your relationship to your child if you have a positive attitude about the payments.

For the person making payments, a positive attitude translates into the joy of helping to provide. If you can trust the other parent to use the money wisely and are not a stickler about the use of every penny; if you can feel the money is going toward the child's personal enrichment and well-being; then some of the sacrifice you are making becomes more endurable. Even if you have questions about how the money is used, concentrating on your ability to fulfill your financial responsibility to your offspring is redeeming for you. It's something you can be proud of. It will also soften some of the hurt or guilt you may feel because of separation from your children. In a way, your support reflects your caring and your presence; at least it helps for you to think of it that way.

For the parent receiving payments, trying to receive them with appreciation also is redeeming. The parent can point out positively for the offspring, if they are old enough to understand, that the other parent is giving money out of love for them. A mature attitude prevents fashioning the child support issue into one more barrier to happy adjustment. Trying to treat in trust what really may be given more sacrificially than you think is both heroic and upbuilding.

Take it from an eight-year-old I know. Her mother told her about the father sending two hundred dollars a month. The father didn't visit her very often, but she was aware that he sent money. One day she beamed proudly and said to me, "My daddy sends me hundreds of dollars every month, to help take care of me!"

Whether you should tell your children in terms of dollar amounts and specifics is something to play by ear. But I think this girl's mother and father had a good thing going in the way child support was looked upon and treated.

If a child support payment is not made, what then? You might talk privately with the other parent about it. If this doesn't bring results or the promise of results, discuss with your attorney if you feel best. All the while, keep the matter between you and the parent. Don't involve the children. Don't try to use visiting privileges as a means of forcing payments, at least not without careful consideration of the possible effects on your offspring—or until every other recourse has been taken. Why? Because you will only hurt the children by creating a new feeling that all is not well, by placing the children in the middle, by breeding more guilt, inadequacy, and insecurity. Besides, in your state, child support and visitation may be two separate things, by law, to prevent your using one to effect the other.

If you are the person making the payments and find yourself genuinely unable to make one, do the other parent the courtesy of discussing it. Don't discuss it with your children. For the same reasons shared above. If the amount of your payments is an increasing problem, you may have to talk with your attorney about what can be done to reduce them; probably though, only a reduction of your income or other unusual circumstance will warrant the amount being reduced. Sorry, but it is true; courts consider support payments as something that comes off the top of your income, like taxes.

The great hope is that even if, for whatever reason, you find yourself in the courtroom again, all parties involved will keep the well-being of the children in mind. It goes back to our discussion in Chapter 5: please don't use your offspring as pawns for advantage or drag them into the middle. And if for some reason you find it necessary to discuss support payments or visitation privileges with your children, do it without put-down of the other parent.

Keeping such matters between yourself and the other parent may be more of a problem if you have preteen or teenaged children. There may be more reasons to discuss some things openly, but with the same supportive attitude. Preteens and teenagers may express more resentments openly. These can be tough to deal with. They may be more judgmental. They may blame the departed parent, or blame you that he or she left.

On the other hand, if you have a teen, he or she may be able to share in your pain more, and help lessen it. You'll need to allow your teen to exercise some personal decision-making power, too, commensurate with age and maturity and whether a matter directly touches the youth's life. Don't push him or her to the background. Don't retreat to the authoritative role, with something like, "Shut up, now. It's my concern, not yours!" Nothing could be more cruel or off the track. Especially if your teen is taking it all very hard anyway.

As long as neither you nor your ex-spouse marry again, things may be complicated enough for the children. If someday you should remarry, you will want to keep in mind that your children will have some kind of relationship with your new husband or wife. If you do not have custody, the responsibilities in your new marriage may affect how much time you can spend with your offspring. Also, your new marriage introduces a new series of adjustments for them. They now must relate to you in a double family context. You'll need to be patient and supportive of them, and of your new spouse. You will want to include your new spouse in any decisions about your children relating to you, so that he or she will not feel left out. You may reserve final say-so for yourself, about some matters, but you don't want to shut your new spouse out or create resentment because of your "split world" situation.

If you are the parent who has custody of the children, you'll have enough everyday adjustments between the new spouse and your offspring to deal with. Try to avoid allowing the relationship with the visiting parent to become a bone of contention for your new spouse. Again, as much as possible, include the new spouse in decisions relating to visitation of the offspring or to the other parent.

It may be unthinkable at first, but in the long run it will be most freeing for all concerned if the time arrives when you all can operate like friends. All along the way your goal is to spare your children as much damaging trauma as possible. You can't shield them from every hurt or bitterness, but you want to give them more than a tarnished self-image or a load of guilt and insecurity!

Guilt! At the beginning of this chapter I promised more about that, so here it is. Let me tell you about a seventeen-year-old girl whose parents had been divorced a decade. As she and I talked I picked up signals of self-blame, so I said: "I want to say something very important: you are in no way to blame for the separation and divorce of your parents. You were the child when it happened; you've been busy growing up since then. *They* were the adults. *They* made their choices apart from you. They loved you, I'm sure of that, because I happen to know them. But they did what they felt they had to do, at the time they divorced, and they did it apart from any influences of yours. You are in *no way* to blame. You can believe that with all your heart.''

She burst into a long, steady stream of tears of relief from all those years of dyked-up guilt and lowered self-image!

Assure your children that your divorce (or separation) is in no way their fault. Say it! ''It's not your fault. You are not to blame in any way. I know you don't understand fully, but maybe someday you will understand better. Meanwhile, we want to help each other. And we don't want it to hurt you any more than it has to.''

We assume that all kinds of things will be figured out by our young ones. Maybe because we don't like facing things squarely with them, ourselves. It hurts us too much. But they need to hear us say they are not to blame. We need to tell them they have done all they could do to make us happy and to fulfill their responsibility as children, that they are not responsible for *our* decisions. We need to say this. Not oversay it, but say it when needed. You can be sure it is needed.

Nevertheless, you can trust your children to work through some of their hurt. Children do have resources for surviving these things. Once, in desperation for my son, I sought out a member of the clergy, who said to me: ''Children are tough! They can survive, not without pain, but they can survive. Sometimes they survive things like divorce better than we adults.''

ABOUT VISITATION

Child visitation! In all my personal experience there is nothing so draining of energy and sometimes trying of spirit. Nothing puts you more quickly in the company of other estranged parents!

I suppose there is some strength in that for us—in the fact that everwhere, everyday, children are visiting with a divorced parent. Everywhere, everyday, parents who have custody of children prepare the children to be visited. If you are a parent, this won't take away the anxiety you feel for your progeny, but it does put you immediately in touch with some others. A little of the loneliness is lessened.

What I want to share about child visitation is from hard experience. I am convinced there are some ways to lessen our children's pain and even to turn their experience of a broken home and visiting parents into a power for nurture. I share gladly what I feel is valid help for a parent-from-a-distance or a parent-without-a-spouse.

1. *With regular visiting times a child often gets more actual time with a parent than he or she might get otherwise.* How many children would give anything for just thirty minutes alone with Mom or Dad? Yet many children of divorced parents get the better part of a whole day, perhaps, with one of their parents, on a sustained, even though spaced-out basis. If we assume that the parent is "there" intensely enough to relate with satisfaction and enjoyment, they may be getting above average solo time with a parent.

2. *Quality is therefore most important, not quantity.* Two hours may be better than six if in that pair of hours you really give your attention and love. You visiting parents know what I'm saying. Remember the times when you felt a visit went empty for you both? The resentment you carried away with you didn't help any either. It didn't help any more than the resentment you may have absorbed from your child.

Might it be better, then, to consider cutting back the length of time together? At least for a while? Would it be kinder to come only every other week instead of weekly? Or monthly instead of bimonthly? Whatever the details of

101

time, don't leave the decision to your offspring. Decide, in consultation with the other parent if possible, and in line with your own intuitions, then do it. Act with affirmation of your child, in your eyes and in your words. Then proceed with confidence to explain that you think both of you will enjoy the times together if you make more exciting and meaningful plans for fewer days. Work to make your visits really super!

3. *Evaluating what you are doing together helps.* Is each visit really meaningful? At least most of the visits? Meaningful to whom? Are you always doing things only *you* enjoy? If so, what can you do that your child enjoys? If you're doing things your child enjoys but these are boring for you, are there other things you can do together? What can you do that might be more enjoyable to you and still helpful or fun to your child? What can you do to bring the two of you closer? Are there times when you don't need to "do" anything super?

During the time I visited my preschool son regularly, he and his mother lived in a different city. We used to love just going to a park occasionally and sitting under a tree and reading a book together, or even taking a short nap. Our communication was more by way of involvement in relaxing experiences, more nonverbal at times than verbal. I also recall times when we visited friends of mine who had children, or went to see Grandma.

Taking time to evaluate will result in clarity about what works best. It will add a variety that will spark visits a little more. So don't drift along; take a close look occasionally.

4. *Treating holiday or special day visits with concern for the child is important.* If you want to split your child down the middle, then hassle over special days with the other parent. Hassle with no regard for anything but your own wishes. Sure you want little George or Alice with you for Santa's visit or for turkey and trimmings at

Thanksgiving; sure you want to be there when that birthday party takes place. Understandably. But you'll be loved and valued for time to come if you avoid a tug-of-war.

A workable schedule of visits should have been arrived at for special days in your custody agreement. But there needs to be an ongoing concern for the child that overrides court decrees or who has what rights. There needs desperately to be a parental spirit of give-and-take for the sake of the child, with no abnormal fuss over details!

Respect the child's feelings, for one thing. Would your son or daughter rather, for some personal reason (such as being with friends), spend a birthday at home? Or even this Christmas in one place or the other? Does your child reflect that a week away, during a special season particularly, is just too long not to expect homesickness?

On the other hand, you can't let every whim of a child dictate everything. Besides, some balking may be difficulty in making the transition from being with one parent to being with the other. Patience and understanding will reveal this is the case, often. Once a visit is under way, the balking usually lessens. It may help to explain to a balking child why it is important for you to have him or her with you for a special occasion, but without making the child feel guilty for balking: "I understand how you feel, but it does mean a lot to me to have you for this special holiday time. How can we work it out?"

There may come a day, however, when you must decide to cut a visit back or to cut it short, to help heal the child's hurts at that particular time. The key becomes what really is best for the child—and most healing. You and your feelings are important, too. But what's best and healing for your offspring is uppermost in your heart, isn't it? And when you decide and act responsibly you spare your offspring the terror of having to shoulder overly much responsibility for the relationship with you.

5. *Your attitude is the key to lessening the discomfort of coming or going.* Is your mind clear of resentments, so that you don't fall into the trap of using a son or daughter or the visit to "get back" at your ex? Why *are* you continuing to visit? Not, I hope, because you have harbored hopes of someday patching it all up with your spouse, and the visit is a chance to possibly get to see him or her, as you pick up the offspring. Not that, at least, unless circumstances are such that there really is reason to believe the relationship will flower again and you are convinced that is best for all of you. Not, I hope, because you feel guilty not visiting.

In whatever ways you honestly can, do you try to make your child's other parent a beautiful person in his or her eyes? Do you approach the visits positively? Do you speak with genuine confidence when having to miss planned visits? Do you assure that the next one can be looked forward to? Are you flexible enough that you can skip a visit or two when it is inconvenient for the other parent or the child? Do you refuse to let any trailing sense of guilt or regret sneak into your relationship? Do you voice your positive support and love for the child often? Do you answer as honestly and openly as you can the important questions he or she shares—or respond with empathy to feelings expressed? Are you able to relate to the child with the firmness and guidance expected of a parent's love? Do you refuse to treat the child so special that your treatment borders on unreal and works against character development? Do you refuse to allow the child psychologically to get between you and the other parent? Are you on guard against allowing your offspring to use situations that appear to contradict what the other parent desires? And if you are the parent who has custody, do you refuse to pump your child with questions when he or she returns from a visit with the other parent?

6. *You divorced parents can lend strength and depth*

to a child's experience of life during the years of visitation. If you are a visiting parent, you may have wondered whether you should step out of the picture altogether, for the sake of your young one. In my opinion, it doesn't necessarily follow that the void created by breaking off contact until mature years would be less painful for the child or more conducive to happiness than having a come-and-go parent. Backing away for a time or times could be healthier for offspring or parent. But fading out altogether could create feelings of having been forsaken, or raise the question, "What's wrong with me that Daddy (Mother) doesn't come to see me?" I guess I am thinking of the brave little boy who once said to me, "Maybe if I give Daddy a present, he will come see me more." He felt the long absences between the father's visits very keenly. In wondering why, he was naturally looking within, since no other explanations were understandable at a feeling level. The equation worked out: Daddy's gone = Daddy doesn't like me = there's something I've done = there's something wrong with me.

Feelings of having been forsaken or feelings of guilt will have to be faced and dealt with by parent and child someday, and that could be painful, too. Walking out of the offspring's life could also result in harsh feelings of guilt for the parent; and it *could* turn out to be as much a way of running from a parent's own hurt as a noble sacrifice on the parent's part.

The truth is, though, no one has the right or emotional basis for sitting in judgment on any parent. The decision to maintain constant contact or to break it off until later years has to be made by each parent on the basis of what he or she knows of the situation and the children—as well as on the basis of the parent's best self-knowledge.

Both the parent-from-a-distance and the parent who has custody need to be aware that they cannot expect to be perfect in every respect as parents. In spite of the best intentions and hopes—or in spite of all these suggestions—you won't be perfect. With lots of love and intrepidity, joy *can* happen for you and your progeny.

As a Christian, I can't help wondering whether some of the children Jesus took into his arms were from broken homes. Jesus reflects the divine love for all children. Whatever your religious persuasion, you can believe that God wants to forge the same kind of meaning and wholeness for your young ones that you desire. God loves them. Their survival doesn't depend on you alone. They have durable resources at work—and so does God.

A POSTCRIPT: If your offspring are older, there are different adjustments to make. I know a college student who experienced quite a lot of stress when her parents divorced. "Going home" became traumatic; she never was clear about where "home" was after that. Eventually she solved the psychological problem by thinking of both residences of her parents as "home," visiting one or the other from time to time. The parents had to realize on rather short notice that their daughter was now "on her own."

In another case I'm familiar with, a couple divorced after many years of marriage. The burden was upon them to adjust to their grown son's need to see them separately or to have them visit at his home at different times. They finally grasped the cruelty of expecting the son to be the go-between for the two of them. Once they did, the problems for the son were not as great.

11
If You Think
of Marrying Again

NOTICE THE TITLE of this chapter—*if* you think of marrying again. Fact: nothing under heaven or on earth requires another marriage. You may not be prevented from it, but you don't need to feel pressured into remarrying. You're free not to marry, to choose to seek happiness apart from matrimony. Probably you *will* want to think of marrying, though. Most persons who divorce eventually consider marrying again.

You were hurt deeply the first time around. The six-million-dollar question is: Are you ready for another time around? Alas, some people fall prematurely into a second marriage, or even into a third. They are into it up to here before they have had an adequate opportunity to evaluate where they have been and where they are in relation to the first marriage. Before they have had time to collect emotions, before they have filtered through what they are looking for in another marriage, they are pulled into a second marriage rather than moving into it thoughtfully. The result: they are on a failure-go-round.

Consider a few types:

1. *The married-to-marriage type*. The marrying kind! The thought behind the remarriage may be, "I'm just not complete without marriage." You might call it the case of

the "it's just the thing to do" type. The divorced person concludes that . . . well, the thing to do is to get married again. Obviously something's awry. One real possibility is the person's inability to stand alone, a lack of basic security and self-identity needed to be his or her own person. The inability to resist being taken in by every hint of marriage or the need to be fulfilled by it. There is a lack of personal self-appreciation, and an independence strong enough to enable a healthy contribution to the success of a marriage relationship.

On the other hand, the married-to-marriage type could have opposite characteristics. A marriage partner is needed to express dominance, as an avenue to setting one's self up over a family, especially the spouse of the family. Like a mother hen and brood, or a queen bee and hive, this person is in charge. And in need of professional help!

I'm thinking here of a still young woman I'll call Bonnie. She has been married three times. Her decisions to marry in each case, even the first time, were made on short notice. Just a matter of months for one marriage; for another only two or three months; for the third, only a few weeks. No amount of reasoning could dissuade her from tying the knot each time. No one tried to discourage her the first time. It was assumed she could find happiness even though her spouse was only a six-month acquaintance. But the second and third times, eyebrows and questions were raised by her family and by me. Each time she came through with a convincing case for being "sure" this was for her. Each time her marriage lasted less than two years; one, less than six months. In one case she described her courtship as "He swept me off my feet." In all three marriages, she said, "I'm just the marrying kind!" She might also have called herself . . .

2. *The drifter type.* Some divorced persons appear to be "bait" for a trapped, possibly unwanted second

marriage—or third. It's as though they are looking for another failure. When another person reaches out with affection or attention, they seem helpless to resist—as though they are drifting into the clutches of fate, and not because they are under any control of others. They lack the control and integrity to know what they want, or to resist what is offered or pressed upon them. They not only are very dependent, they have a low self-image. They're looking for someone to solve their problems, take away their hurt, and determine their future for them. They may drift into a marriage, drift right through a divorce and into another marriage, and then another divorce. Usually each marriage develops from a convenient and "easy" relationship. Rarely does the passive type file for a divorce. When rejected, there is still no taking a hint that something is amiss personally, no ability to take control. No ability to assert one's self, only more drifting.

Once I was asked to remarry a man and a woman who both had been divorced. We were hampered in premarital counseling because of distance. I felt uneasy, heaven forgive, but decided to officiate because the woman was the daughter of a friend of some years back. The whole family felt confident about the marriage. In fact, I realized too late that the father was the big push behind the wedding. In one conference close to the time of the ceremony I noticed the bride-to-be was extremely nervous. I asked her if she felt all right about the step she was about to take.

"I guess so," she said. Then she assured me she was just "shaky" about remarrying. I proceeded with the wedding, that next week, but from the moment she stood up with her husband-to-be, she had a "scared rabbit" look in her eyes. It was the look of being caught in a tight grip, of being too scared to get loose from it. I've never come so close to halting a wedding midstream in all my twenty-five years of tying or retying knots!

Yet it's true that a divorce will sometimes push a drifter type to become more self-assertive and independent. The need is for counseling, to enable more active participation in the choice of a matrimonial mate, and to avoid picking or being picked by losers.

3. *The carbon-copy-seeker type*. The classic case, this—of the divorced person who "just happens" to meet someone who is a duplicate, in too many ways, of the former spouse. The resemblance may be physical or personality-wise. Because the person isn't able to separate self emotionally from the earlier marriage, she or he seeks to preserve the marriage by duplicating it. It could spell trouble for the new union if this occurs!

The problem often is that the trap is set for the carbon-copy-seeker type in such a subtle, unknowing way. Emotionally he or she may "see" in a prospective mate certain characteristics—physical or psychological—that remind of the former spouse. But watch out! These may find their familiarity rooted still deeper in other past relationships. For example, a past acquaintance of mine, an only male child, woke up one day married to his older "sister." Not literally, but emotionally. The new spouse's smile and way of shifting her eyes were almost identical with those of the real-life sister. What a revelation when he realized this and that the first time around he had married a carbon of his mother!

We all look for familiar ways in others—ways that make us feel comfortable with them—without telling ourselves that we are looking for them. It's possible that men naturally seek qualities in a mate reminiscent of their mothers or other significant women in their lives. Women may tend to marry men who remind them of father or brother figures they have known. These tendencies are not necessarily bad in themselves, unless they blind to other needs or expectations. And with luck enough, the carbon-copy spouse may be of a different temperament or greater maturity in some key ways, so that the new union may survive. Nevertheless, this type is playing a risky game! Some real work in counseling is the prescribed safeguard. The person needs to achieve a degree of objective detachment from the former marriage and to "bury" the original who is superficially being copied. At least, enough to bring the duplicating tendencies into conscious enough focus to be able to enter more thoughtfully into the new relationship.

4. *The "I'm looking for someone different" type.* Line up anger or hurt as the prime movers behind this type. Opposite to the carbon-copy seeker this type is determined not to repeat the pain and failures of the first matrimonial venture. No risking rejection again! The way to be *sure,* goes the unconscious "reasoning," is to find someone with qualities and characteristics opposite those of the first spouse. Physical appearances may be involved: going from brunet to blond, from slender to stout, from small features to larger or larger to smaller, from beautiful to "just plain." Personal characteristics are involved: going from extrovert to introvert, from sophistication to down-to-earth, from dependent to independent, from idealistic to practical, from religious to agnostic, etc. Obviously what's needed by this type is greater self-understanding, as well as ample time for that to come about.

Caution here though: not every choice of a "different" mate within second marriages spells failure. I more often hear people say of second wives or husbands, "She (he) is so different from the first wife (husband)" than I hear "She (he) is so much like So-and-So." And the different physical or personal makeup of a second-choice spouse could be precisely because some thought *has* been put into the selection.

It would help, as it would help for the other types, for

the "I'm looking for someone different" type to list some priority questions to guide in the selection of a new partner. What *personal* qualities or values are desired in a spouse-to-be, whether these are like or not like the former spouse? Counseling will help achieve enough understanding to be objective, as well as reveal whether and why the person may be running from accepting the divorce. If so, what to do about it?

5. *The triangle type.* Triangles are common enough. A second partner in marriage is chosen before the first partner is divorced. A lot of risks and dangers can be tagged to triangle involvements and the marriages they spawn. The person who breaks the commitment of a marriage to become involved with a third person can ask questions like: Why has the other party been sought out, the affair held? Is this a case of being in love? Or has the unhappiness of the existing marriage driven the person to the relationship? Will the new relationship survive in marriage? Is it guilt-free enough? Does it have integrity enough? Some genuine soul-searching is needed.

It's possible you were the victim of a triangle involvement. Your spouse may have left you for another. If so, you have scars from this; those scars can be an encouragement against hasty involvements of your own, whether your ex-spouse's venture worked out or not.

Those who are party to a triangle may be so far out on a limb in the new relationship that it's hard to back up and be objective about it. Underscore the need to do so.

6. *The rebounder type.* You know this one: rejection so keenly felt and insecurity so real that a person bounces into the arms of another. Different from the triangle type in that the partner chosen was not even in the running for marriage prior to the divorce, this type makes a hasty decision and the person married probably is just as insecure. Total it up to new hurt and rejection—for someone. When the dust settles and things are thought

112

through, the rebounder may decide that the second marriage was not undertaken in good faith. Grand total: another divorce!

You have guessed correctly: for the rebounder the antidote to hasty marriage is time and more time—to grieve the hurt out and think through the divorce. Time to get over rejection and get mind and heart together. Time to become secure enough to genuinely fall in love again.

Meet a fellow I'll call Tom. He was deeply in love with his wife, a raving Texas beauty! Just two years of marriage and the girl jilted him, abruptly. It was like hitting Tom with the Dallas Cowboy Stadium! In just six weeks after the divorce he staggered to the altar with a schooldays girlfriend who had her eyes full of Tom for years. In just one week Tom was in his attorney's office filing for a second divorce! He told his new bride during the honeymoon that he had never stopped loving the Texas beauty!

7. *The "let's be practical" type.* Note the kinship to the married-to-marriage type. But the slant of thinking is pragmatic. "It just makes sense that I get married again," is the refrain here. Or, "Why not? He (she) is a fine person. He (she) is alone, too. So why not?" Sometimes just because people have known each other for a long time, maybe even from childhood, there is a pull to be practical when considering remarriage to each other.

Practical marriages are not uncommon with some elderly persons I have known, or with younger adults who face tight financial budgets. Remarrying offers greater economic security or a solution to loneliness, verbalized or not.

What a tragic ending to this story about a shy man in his late fifties whose health wasn't too sound and whose loneliness overwhelmed him. In need of a housekeeper after his wife divorced him, he managed to persuade a widow he knew to marry him within months after the divorce. Just six months later, he was left alone again, when his wife walked off with the contents of his joint bank account.

Sure! A relationship can grow. Two people who need each other can bring companionship to a marriage. Love can flower. One can be fortunate. But the risks are there, in large measure. At least two questions beg to be raised: Is there enough compatibility to spice the arrangement? How do the partners feel about the absence of any conversations between them about love?

8. *The "I want a parent for my children" type.* A noble desire this, to heal a torn family by marrying again. If you are a parent, that desire may be partial grounds for looking for a suitable mate. But don't let it supersede the need for sound spouse qualities in the partner you select. If you are a mother, you may lament that a son doesn't have an everyday father model or "a male hand" to discipline him. If you are a father, you may lament the lack of a mother to "love" your offspring. In either case, you can succeed in discovering a spouse who will fill both parental and spouse roles, provided you face squarely: Do you love this person whose hand you propose to take in marriage? Do you love your children enough to want to provide them with the security of knowing that you, too, are happy in the marriage? Can you be happy in it? Will you be able to trust this parent and spouse-to-be to fulfill both roles? Will she or he be wife or husband first, parent second? Will you be able to let your children go enough, eventually at least, to allow the stepparent to fulfill both roles? Will you be able to let the new spouse into your family circle as a parent? Will your children allow it? What openness or resistance is there to this marriage from deep within you? from within your offspring? What attitudes in the spouse and parent-to-be are good for forming family attitudes about discipline, togetherness,

basic values? Which are compatible with your own? Which would be detrimental to the marriage or to family? Over the long pull, can you expect that you will all grow together as a family? And will your relationship to your husband or wife grow enough to fulfill you? fulfill your spouse?

It's possible too that a person may marry because he or she is fond of someone else's children. Similar questions apply concerning the stepparent's ability to become spouse as well as parent; to be patient enough to grow into the parental role; to be adult enough to be spouse as well as parent. If both spouses have children, the possibility for complications—and added responsibilities— multiply. And then there are the problems that relate to a visiting parent—or to being one yourself if you don't have custody. How well will your new spouse-to-be adjust to the realities of child visitation?

The road to a "what's mine is yours and what's yours is mine" family unity could travel through a lot of headaches. Only time will tell how well it works out. But a careful examination of feelings, motivations, and expectations of parents and children, and talking these over openly will help avoid conflicting scripts for the new marriage and the enlarged family. It can help give you confidence in the direction of going ahead, postponing, or jumping in and trying again!

9. *The "let's try it first" type.* I include this type because divorced persons who come into the live-in arrangement before trying marriage again may do so precisely because they are *not* ready for a second time around. Involvement in a nonmarriage is premature for the same reasons that involvement in a marriage would be. They may want the conveniences, the security, the relationship of a marriage arrangement without that "piece of paper" which makes it binding, without the

responsibility that public scrutiny through a wedding brings, without the faith responsibility that exchange of vows implies.

Some persons entering an LTA (living together arrangement) may genuinely be in love; for a few, the arrangement may seem to produce enough happiness, for even quite some time. But there are questions to ask. What exactly are the reasons why a full commitment is *not* being sought by one or the other or both partners? Why is it that one or the other wants marriage but is refused? Answering in specifics, honestly, can put the situation in perspective. Sincere feelings, fears, "reasons" can be shared. Talking with a trusted counselor would be ideal. Do the specifics say anything about any promise of a truly satisfying relationship? Is there promise it will last? Do the specifics provide adequate nurturing ground for a caring, secure relationship? Do they reveal sufficient freedom from guilt, irresponsibility, insecurity, and the ghosts of the past, sufficient even for the noncommitted, intimate relationship of an LTA?

If either partner involved in a live-in-arrangement has children, I would hope this fact alone would discourage it. To live-in when only one's self is involved is one thing. But to live-in and bring in one's offspring puts the decision in a different light because any joy and pain of the relationship are shared. Not to cause a child any further pain after the pain of a broken marriage is reason enough to be cautious.

Then we have to go back to the question of shame and regret. I know one or two couples who seem to have found security of a sort in their "try it first" relationship. So I want to "put the monkey" back on the shoulders of those contemplating a live-in. Your arrangement eventually will be public. How do you really feel about that? Will you be willing to pay the price of your feelings? Will the arrangement cause you remorse of conscience? Will

116

you be gaining as much as losing? Will it provide the best opportunity for the divine working in you?

10. *The another-round-in-the-matrimonial-battle type.* In this case, a divorce is more of a solution to a round in the matrimonial battle and the persons divorced marry *each other* again when the round ends. The divorce is a way of settling temporarily the ills of the marriage, or at least of providing respite from those ills. Neither spouse can tolerate the emotional tearing and risks involved in a permanent separation, however. So they remarry each other.

If you are thinking of remarrying your ex-spouse, or if your ex-spouse is putting pressure on you to remarry, you owe it to yourself to rethink what you really want over the long pull. If your divorce is final, should you let the marriage die forever? Or is there hope that a remarriage to each other *will* result in greater joy than before? Have you in the time separated grown enough to promise that some attitudes and ways of behavior vital to the health of the marriage might now be more mature? What about your spouse? And do you really love him or her?

It's very possible that enough change can come about if separation is long enough before remarriage is attempted. Going through the fire does encourage the emergence of a new you! And if motivation is strong, then with counseling the separation and divorce could turn out to be the best thing that ever happened to your marriage (and remarriage)—and to your offspring if you have them. But the caution is that you not—after all you've been through—put yourself in a position of having to repeat all over again the hurt and the pain. Think, pray, proceed thoughtfully as well as emotionally.

That last sentence applies whether you remarry your ex-spouse or whomever! If you are thinking of rewards missed the first time around, some guideline questions that will help beam you toward success beckon.

1. *Am I squared away emotionally?* Have you accepted emotionally that the other marriage is dead, that you "are no longer kin to her (him)"? Have you grieved enough? Have you taken time to feel the pain so that the pain will not plague your second time around? Have the stages, the process of grief been sufficiently completed and dealt with? Have you given up all the "ghosts" you need to give up?

2. *Am I free from within?* Are you whole enough for remarriage? Have you put enough pieces in place with understanding of yourself and who you are, and what your strengths and weaknesses are? Are you at peace with yourself? Are you comfortable enough with you?

3. *Am I able to trust others enough just yet?* When you have been hurt this could be crucial. It may take time really to be able to trust again emotionally. Until you feel you can, it may be questioned whether it is time to become involved in another marriage.

4. *Am I taking my time so I will act free from pressures?* Not only pressures of time, but of people, circumstances, practicality, whatever. To put it another way, are you "with it" in any decision to remarry? Is this *your* decision, actively and joyfully entered into? apart from outside pressures?

5. *What possible liabilities and assets am I carrying into another marriage?* What about children? Child support? Special health concerns? These need not be unbearable burdens, as such; the question is whether you have considered them objectively enough. The question is whether the intended spouse knows about and accepts the "burdens" enough to want to share in them. And what positive assets, personal or otherwise, do you offer in remarriage? What does your spouse-to-be bring to remarriage?

6. *Where am I faith-wise in all this?* What does God have to say about your thoughts about remarriage? If you

are a person of faith, you will search mind and heart for an open, honest answer to this one. Along with a faith commitment to the new marriage, you may have need to wrestle with the question of what your church, synagogue, or religious group teaches about marriage, divorce, and remarriage. How do you feel about what is taught? Is there freedom from guilt feelings about the past marriage, the divorce, the remarriage? Have you conferred with a minister, priest, or rabbi? Is there evidence of a growing relationship between you and God and a promise of spiritual help for a new marriage?

7. *Can I trust myself to love another and commit myself to that person?* There can come a time when you find that you are ready to trust not only another person but yourself to contribute love to another relationship. You may wonder if you will be able to sustain marital vows over the long pull. Much depends on how well you have weaned yourself from the other time, before God, and in your own eyes. If you are hesitant, it is understandable. If you are cautious, that can be good. Are you ready to trust yourself to making another marriage work?

8. Special for parents: *How do my offspring fit into the picture?* All the questions raised under the "I want a parent for my children" type are significant and related. To the parents reading this: serious discussions between the parent-to-be and the parent are needed to clear up as many problems as possible in advance, to clarify false expectations, to reinforce valid ones. Surely if you feel that another marriage would bring hurt to your children, you cannot consent to it. Surely if your new spouse does not want to be nor feel himself or herself equipped to be a parent, he or she would not conscientiously enter into a marriage demanding that role. And if you think of marrying another parent, surely you will want to weigh carefully your feelings about your expected role.

On the other hand, in spite of some adjustments and

problems, is there a degree of promise for joy and happiness for all of you? Assuming the offspring are old enough to understand, have you, will you and your new spouse-to-be bring them into your decision-making too? Yet, will you decide for your own fulfillment as well as theirs?

There may be other questions to ask yourself if you think of marrying again. If you do want to marry, this is an indication that you believe in marriage, that your past experiences have not spoiled marriage for you. What you can prize is adequate time and space for sorting out any pulls or pushes from within. You don't want to be led into a hasty, unenlightened decision. You owe it to yourself to make your new venture in marriage a free, confident step of faith, with every hope—this time—of bliss and blessing!

12
One Step More

WE HAVE DISCUSSED and bared together quite a gamut of emotions and emotional experiences: humiliation, anger, dread, depression, grief, insecurity, parental love, guilt, loneliness, among others. As you have known unwanted separation or divorce, crucial to working your way through each of these has been your ability to face the demise of your marriage and to let your partner in marriage "die." It has been important to accept that you are no longer legally responsible to or for the other, just as the other is no longer legally responsible to or for you.

At several points, but particularly in Chapter 6 on grief, I encouraged you to thus release your ex-spouse. If you have been able to do this, you have done a great deal as one who has suffered the uninvited death of a marriage. But for your complete healing, I now encourage you to do more.

Even though you may feel you have "buried" the former partner for keeps, now can you take a final, more positive step? Can you resurrect the partner to life? I encourage you to bring your ex-spouse out of the closet of your emotions and consciously and subconsciously release the person to life. Release him or her to happiness and joy, to good health and good fortune. It is not enough just to say, "I wish him (her) no ill; I hold no hate for him (her) in my heart." To truly face up to unwanted separation or divorce requires that you hold good in your heart for the other. Wish your ex-spouse well and whole and happy—happy in another marriage, happy in personal pursuits and aspirations. Imagine the ex-spouse right now, as you read perhaps; imagine happiness and joy for her or him.

You may or may not have regular contact with your ex-spouse, if any at all. Your ex-spouse may or may not be positive toward you. But no matter. Whatever the feelings or outlook of your ex-spouse, give him or her up positively to abundant life and to God's care.

Difficult? Oh, yes! But it is *the only way!*

If you are a person of Christian faith, you will find motivation and power for this kind of positive releasing in the resurrection of Jesus. His resurrection is both the power and parable of life and living for those who follow him in faith. Jesus did not remain in the tomb of death; he came out of death into life! You do not want your former partner in marriage, nor yourself, to remain forever entombed by the death of your marriage and all the emotional tearing it has produced, either. By faith, with Jesus' loving and powerful help, you seek new life—not more death—for those who may have despitefully used you. You are part of the continuing resurrection parable of life out of death, as you refuse to be bound by hatred or destructive forces or emotions. By faith, Jesus' resurrection means that as in you, so for your ex-spouse, God is bringing life-giving good out of the deceased marriage.

Of Christian persuasion or not, if you are a person of faith, a positive faith release is in itself new life for you. It will be your healing and wholeness. It will set you truly free. You will be able to sigh a great sigh of the spirit, and to walk into your own future unafraid of anything, confident in the power of life and grace.

You will also have more to give to others. Through your experience of unwanted separation and divorce and by the power of life and grace you have the gift of understanding. You are able to empathize with those who are going through the fire, because you have been through it yourself. You will be a whole lot less judgmental of those who have joined the statistics of divorce, and those who are disappointed or torn in other ways. Because you have known encouragement from people and from God when you most needed it, you will be supportive of others. You can inspire new life in others, including your offspring, because new life has been given to you.

Suggested Readings

Achtemeier, Elizabeth. *The Committed Marriage*. Westminster Press, 1976.

Arnold, William V. *When Your Parents Divorce*. Christian Care Books. Westminster Press, 1980.

Arnold, William V. et al. *Divorce: Prevention or Survival*. Westminster Press, 1977.

Buscaglia, Leo F. *Love*. (A Warm and Wonderful Book About the Largest Experience in Life.) Fawcett Crest, 1972.

Carter, Kay; Thompson, Judy; Brookman, Mary Lou. *Something Shared*. Picnic Press, 1980.

Claypool, John R. *Tracks of a Fellow Struggler: How to Handle Grief*. Word, 1974.

Craig, Sidney D. *Raising Your Child, Not by Force but by Love*. Westminster Press, 1982.

Dodson, Fitzhugh. *How to Parent*. New American Library, 1971.

Gardner, Richard A. *The Boys and Girls Book About Divorce*. Bantam Books, 1971.

———. *The Parents' Book About Divorce*. Bantam Books, 1977.

Grollman, Earl A., ed. *Explaining Divorce to Children*. Beacon Press, 1969.

Hauck, Paul A. *Marriage Is a Loving Business*. Westminster Press, 1977.

———. *Overcoming Depression*. Westminster Press, 1973.

———. *Overcoming Frustration and Anger*. Westminster Press, 1974.

Krantzler, Mel. *Creative Divorce: A New Opportunity for Personal Growth*. M. Evans Co., 1974.

Kübler-Ross, Elisabeth. *Death: The Final Stage of Growth*. Prentice-Hall, 1975.

L'Abate, Luciano and Bess. *How to Avoid Divorce*. (Help for Troubled Marriages.) John Knox Press, 1977.

Levine, James A. *Who Will Raise the Children?* J. B. Lippincott Co., 1976.

Mason, Robert L., Jr., and Jacobs, Carrie I. *How to Choose the Wrong Marriage Partner and Live Unhappily Ever After*. John Knox Press, 1978.

Oates, Wayne E. *Your Particular Grief*. Westminster Press, 1981.

Olson, Dr. Ken. *The Art of Hanging Loose in an Uptight World*. Fawcett Crest, 1975.

Powell, John. *Why Am I Afraid to Tell Who I Am?* Argus Communications Co., 1969.

Roosevelt, Ruth, and Lofas, Jeanette. *Living in Step*. (Step Parenting.) McGraw-Hill Book Co., 1977.

Shedd, Charlie W. *Letters to Karen: On Keeping Love in Marriage*. Abingdon Press, 1966.

———. *Letters to Philip: On How to Treat a Woman*. Doubleday & Co., 1968.

Tournier, Paul. *The Meaning of Persons*. Harper & Row, 1973.

———. *Reflections: A Personal Guide for Life's Most Crucial Questions*. Westminster Press, 1982.

———. *To Understand Each Other*. John Knox Press, 1967.

Provide for my family

1. To be dependable, responsible

break

2.

3.

4.